ORCHESOGRAPHY

ORCHESOGRAPHY

A TREATISE IN THE FORM OF A DIALOGUE

Whereby all manner of persons may easily acquire and practise the honourable exercise of dancing

BY

THOINOT ARBEAU

Now first translated from the original edition published at Langres, 1588

BY

CYRIL W. BEAUMONT

With a Preface

BY

PETER WARLOCK

One of a series of republications by
Dance Horizons, Incorporated
1801 East 26th Street, Brooklyn, New York 11229

The typography used is that arranged by Cyril W. Beaumont for the first edition of his translation and published by him in London, in 1925.

Library of Congress Catalog Card No. 65-28336

Printed in the United States of America

This *English* Translation of THOINOT ARBEAU'S *Orchésographie* is DEDICATED

To SERGE GRIGORIEFF

In memory of many pleasant hours "behind the scenes" passed in his company,

By

His Friend,

THE TRANSLATOR.

NOTE

WHILE French literature is rich in technical and historical works on dancing of all the great epochs, our own is singularly deficient in this respect. The present volume is the first of a contemplated series designed to provide British students with classical works on dancing which hitherto have not been available in an English translation, or which have become so rare as to be almost unobtainable and then only at a price prohibitive to the average pupil.

The *Orchésographie* of Thoinot Arbeau is a detailed treatise on the society dances in vogue throughout the sixteenth century. It contains practical instructions for dancing the *Basse Danse*, *Pavane*, *Gaillarde*, *Volte*, *Courante*, *Allemande*, *Gavotte*, *Canaries*, *Bouffons*, *Morisque*, *Pavane d'Espagne* and twenty-three varieties of the *Branle*. The late Cecil Sharp has remarked that "it would be difficult to exaggerate the historical importance of his [Arbeau's] treatise, for it contains all the exact knowledge that we have of the dances of the fifteenth and sixteenth centuries." It is certainly the best work on the dances of the period cited, but it is not the sole source of information, for that would be to ignore the works of Robert Copland (*The Maner of dauncynge of Bace daunces after the use of fraunce*, 1521), Fabritio Caroso da Sermoneta (*Il Ballarino*, 1581) and Cesare Negri (*Nuove Inventioni di Balli*, 1604).

The *Orchésographie*, first published at Langres in 1588, was reprinted at Paris by F. Vieweg in 1888, which edition is prefaced with an excellent and erudite introduction by Laure Fonta. The present edition is the first English translation to be published. In fact it is the first complete translation in any language, for although a German rendering, by the professor of dancing Albert Czerwinski, was issued at Danzig in 1878 under the title *Die Tänze des XVI. Jahrhunderts und die alte französische Tanzschule vor Einführing der Menuett*, this does not contain the first part dealing with the playing of the pipe and tabor.

In this English edition, the airs have been transposed into modern musical notation by Mr. Peter Warlock and a system of numbering has been employed to show clearly the distribution of steps to the notes. Again, for the convenience of students, the airs are set horizontally across the page, and not vertically as in the first edition. The translations given of the various quotations from Virgil and Horace are taken from the renderings of T. Phaër and T. Twyne (1573) and Ben Jonson (printed in the edition of his works edited by F. Cunningham, 3 Vols., 1871) respectively. I have added some general notes and an index to facilitate reference.

In conclusion I desire to record my warmest thanks first to my friend Mr. de V. Payen-Payne who, in addition to overlooking the proofs, has afforded me many valuable suggestions and much kindly encouragement; and, secondly, to Mr. Warlock who has also read the proofs and who, throughout the work of translation, generously allowed me to draw freely from the great pool of his knowledge of all that concerns the art of music.

CYRIL W. BEAUMONT.

PREFACE

THE existence of a dance presupposes an appropriate tune, to be sung or played upon an instrument. Apart from dance-tunes (which as often as not were also songs) there was practically no instrumental music prior to the second half of the sixteenth century; and to the development of instrumental music during that period all the elements that were not derived from the methods of vocal polyphonic writing were contributed by dance-forms such as are described in this book. There was, of course, a large amount of vocal dance-music, as is shown by the Pavan for four voices *Belle qui tient ma vie* in the present volume, by the names of traditional dance-tunes which, as Sir Thomas Elyot remarks in *The Governor* (1531), were frequently derived from " the first words of the ditty which the song comprehendeth, whereof the dance was made," and, in a more extended field of composition, by such things as the *Ballets* for five voices of Giovanni Gastoldi (1591) and Thomas Morley (1595)—which were not ballets in the modern sense of the word, but short pieces of a well-defined rhythmical character. But one may say without undue exaggeration that the dance is the specifically instrumental influence in early music. It is invariably associated with, if not actually responsible for, the element of measured tune as distinct from the melodic phrases of contrapuntal music in which all the contributory voices are of equal importance; for in dance-music one voice (or instrument) must predominate over the others and impose a definite metrical structure on the composition.

Thomas Morley, in *A Plaine and Easie Introduction to Practicall Musicke* (1597), after treating of various musical forms such as the motet, the madrigal and the canzonet, states that " the most principall and chiefest kind of musicke which is made without a dittie is the fantasie," and that " the next in gravity and goodnes unto this is called a pavane, a kind of staide musicke, ordained for grave dauncing, and most commonlie made of three straines, whereof everie straine is plaid or sung twice, a straine they make to containe 8. 12. or 16. semibreves as they list, yet fewer than eight I have not seene in any pavan. . . . Also in this you must cast your musicke by foure, so that if you keepe that rule it is no matter how many foures you put in your straine, for it will fall out well enough in the ende, the arte of dauncing being come to that perfection that everie reasonable dauncer wil make measure of no measure, so that it is no great matter of what number you make your strayne." The majority of the Pavans in the *Fitzwilliam Virginal Book*, the most important collection of English dance-music of the late sixteenth and early seventeenth centuries, conform to this plan, though the Pavan quoted by Arbeau, like the well-known *Earle of Salisbury* Pavan of William Byrd, has but two strains. John Dowland published in 1605 a collection of Pavans and other dances of his own composition under the title of *Lachrymae, or Seven Teares, figured in 7 passionate Pavans, set forth for the lute, viols or violins, in 5 parts*, and many notable Pavans by William Byrd, Orlando Gibbons, Thomas Morley, Peter Philips, William Tisdall, Thomas Tomkins, and others are to be found in the *Fitzwilliam Virginal Book*. It is not altogether clear whether the Pavan is of Spanish or of Italian origin, the name being derived by some authorities from *Padovana*, meaning *of Padua*, and by others from *pavone*, on account of a fancied resemblance between the stately movements of the dancers and the spreading of a peacock's tail. The tune known as *The Spanish Pavan*, which was very popular in England towards the end of Queen Elizabeth's reign, was used by the Spanish composer Antonio di Cabezon in 1578 as the subject of a set of variations for the virginals under the title *Pavana italiana*, and some thirty years later it appears as the theme of a set of variations for the virginals by the Dutch composers Sweelinck and Scheidt entitled *Paduana hispania*. It is quite different from the tune of the Spanish Pavan quoted by Arbeau.

The Pavan, which was set in duple or quadruple time, was generally followed by a Galliard, a sprightly dance in triple time of which the tune was sometimes, but by no means invariably, a rhythmic transformation of that of the Pavan preceding it. Morley says : " After every pavan we usually set a galliard (that is, a kind of musicke made out of the other) causing it go by a measure, which the learned cal *trochaicam rationem*, consisting of a long and short stroke successivelie, for as the foote *trochaeus* consisteth of one sillable of two times, and another of one time, so is the first of these two strokes double to the latter: the first being in time of a semibrefe, and the latter of a minime. This is a lighter and more stirring kinde of dauncing than the pavane consisting of the same number of straines, and looke howe manie foures of semibreves you put in the straine of your pavan, so many times sixe minimes must you put in the straine of your galliard. The Italians make their galliardes (which they tearme *saltarelli*) plaine, and frame ditties to them, which in their *mascaradoes* they sing and daunce, and many times without any instruments at all, but in steed of instruments they have Curtisans disguised in mens apparell, who sing and daunce to their owne songes." The word galliard is, of course, derived from the French *gaillard*, meaning lively (Shakespeare refers to the "nimble galliard"), and the dance is said to have originated in the Campagna, where it was known as the Romanesca. In its original form it consisted of five steps and was in consequence sometimes referred to as the Cinque-pas or, in English, sink-a-pace, but towards the end of the sixteenth century many new steps were added to it, and we find Barnabe Riche, in his *Farewell to Militarie Profession* (1581) saying: "Our galliardes are so curious, thei are not for my daunsyng, for thei are so full of trickes and tournes, that he which hath no more but the plaine sinquepace is not better accoumpted of than a verie bungler." John Webster makes an interesting allusion to the galliard in the *Duchess of Malfi* (i., 1) in Antonio's description of the duchess:

> "whilst she speaks,
> She throws upon a man so sweet a look,
> That it were able to raise one to a galliard
> That lay in a dead palsy."

and a much earlier use of the word as a simple adjective is to be found in the *Cook's Tale* of Chaucer:

> "Gaillard he was as Goldfinch in the shawe."

The Alman or Allemande is described by Morley as "a more heavie daunce then this [the galliard] (fitlie representing the nature of the people whose name it carieth) so that no extraordinarie motions are used in dauncing of it. It is made of strains, sometimes two, sometimes three, and everie straine is made by foure, but you must marke that the foure of the pavan measure is in *dupla* proportion to the foure of the *Alman* measure, so that as the usuall Pavane conteineth in a straine the time of sixteene semibreves, so the usuall *Almaine* containeth the time of eight, and most commonlie in short notes. Like unto this is the French *bransle* (which they cal *bransle simple*) which goeth somewhat rounder in time [i.e. quicker] then this, otherwise the measure is all one. The *bransle de poictou* or *bransle double* is more quick in time (as being in a rounde Tripla) but the straine is longer, containing most usually twelve whole strokes. Like unto this (but more light) be the *voltes* and *courantes* which being both of a measure, ar notwithstanding daunced after sundrie fashions, the *volte* rising and leaping, the *courante* travising and running, in which measure also our country daunse is made, though it be daunced after another forme then any of the former. All these be made in straines, either two or three as shall seeme best to the maker, but the *courant* hath twice so much in a straine as the English country daunce." The " courante travising and running " is thus described in Sir John Davies's poem *Orchestra* (1594), one of the earliest books on dancing written in English :

" What shall I name those current traverses,
That on a triple dactyl foot do run
Close by the ground with sliding passages,
Wherein that dance's greatest praise hath won
Which with best order can all orders shun ;
For everywhere he wantonly must range
And turn and wind with unexpected change."

Of the courante, or coranto, the same author says :

" Yet is there one the most delightful kind,
A lofty jumping or a leaping round,
Where arm in arm two dancers are entwin'd,
And whirl themselves with strict embracements bound.
And still their feet an anapest do sound ;
An anapest is all their music's song,
Whose first two feet are short and third is long."

And Shakespeare, in *Henry V.* (iii. 5) refers to these dances together :

" They bid us to the English dancing-schools,
And teach lavoltas high and swift corantos ;
Saying our grace is only in our heels,
And that we are most lofty runaways."

A rhythmic transformation of the Pavan *Belle qui tient ma*

vie by William Byrd, in the form of a Coranto, appears in the *Fitzwilliam Virginal Book.*

The Hey, or Haye, which is mentioned by Clément Marot and Rabelais, is described in the *New English Dictionary* as "a country dance having a winding or serpentine movement, or being of the nature of a reel." John Skelton (*circa* 1530) refers to it in the lines:

> "I cannot let thee the knave to play
> To dauns the hay and run the ray."

and Sir John Davies in the work already quoted speaks of "Rounds and winding Heyes." An interesting figurative use of the phrase "to dance the hay" is found in Hakluyt's *Voyages* (1597): "Through variety of judgements and evill marinership we were faine to dance the hay foure dayes together."

The Morisco, as its name implies, is a dance of Moorish origin which reached Europe by way of Spain. It is connected, though only remotely, with our English Morris dance. (On this point see *The Morris Book* by Cecil Sharp and Herbert MacIlwaine.) Monteverde's famous opera *Orfeo* (1608) concludes with a fine *Moresca* which is in triple time but with a binary accent.

The Matassins is also connected with the Morris. The air quoted by Arbeau, *Les Bouffons*, was used by Dr. John Bull as the theme for a set of variations for the virginals. It bears a striking resemblance to the popular Elizabethan song *John come kiss me now*, on which William Byrd and John Tomkins wrote variations for the virginals. John Webster refers to the Matassins dance at the end of *The White Devil* (v. 6):

> LODOVICO: We have brought you a mask.
> FLAMINEO: A matachin, it seems by your drawn swords.

The method of playing the pipe and tabor will be understood clearly enough from Arbeau's description and the accompanying illustration. There is a portrait of Richard Tarleton, the Elizabethan comedian, with his pipe and tabor in one of the Harleian manuscripts, and the title-page of *Kemps nine daies wonder* (1600) is adorned with a woodcut representing the author dancing his famous morris dance from London to Norwich, "attended on by Thomas Slye his Taberer." Kemp, who was a comedian of Shakespeare's company and the original actor of the part of Dogberry, describes himself in his book as " Head Master of Morrice dancers, High Headborough of Heighs, and only tricker of your trill-lilles and best bell-shangles, between Sion and Mount Surrey." Pipe and tabor is a very ancient combination of instruments, and its use, under the name of whittle and dub, survived in certain parts of England until the beginning of the present century. " The whittle and dub, after they fell into disuse, were superseded by the fiddle, concertina or melodeon," says Cecil Sharp in *The Morris Book*. " Many old Morris men have told us that they gave up dancing when the pipe and tabor were superseded by the fiddle, because they found it impossible to dance to the latter instrument. Probably they missed the rhythmical support of the drum-notes ; but the sound of the pipe and tabor is so distinctive that one can well understand that those who had never heard any other instrument might find it difficult to become reconciled to anything else. The Morris airs have, of course, suffered considerable change in the transference from pipe to fiddle or concertina." An example of the imitation of a drum on the virginals in the manner described by Arbeau may be found in a section of that curious piece of programme-music *Mr. Byrd's Battle* under the title of " The flute and the Droome." It is quoted in Vol. III. of the *Oxford History of Music*.

The name Thoinot Arbeau is in reality an anagram of Jehan Tabourot, a Catholic priest, who was born at Dijon in 1519 and became canon of Langres. He published his *Orchésographie* in 1588, at the age of sixty-nine, having previously issued another book (*Compost et manuel Calendrier par lequel toutes personnes peuvent facilement à prendre et savoir les cours du soleil et de la lune*) which shows him to have been something of an astronomer and mathematician. He had, as we read in the opening paragraph of the *Orchésographie*, already initiated Capriol into the mysteries of astronomical computation before teaching him " the honourable exercise of the dance."

His musical phraseology is sometimes a little obscure, especially in regard to his use of the words *cadence*, *réduction* and *découppement*. *Cadence* is used indifferently for the conclusion of a musical phrase, for the fall of the dancer's feet to the ground which coincides with the conclusion of the phrase, or for " the measure or beat of music, dancing or rhythmic movement," as the *New English Dictionary* defines its English equivalent. *Réduction* appears to mean the substitution of a rest of equal value for a note at some point in an air. *Découppement* seems to correspond to the old English use of the word *division*, as in the common seventeenth-century title " Divisions on a Ground," denoting the embellishment of an air in long notes with florid figuration in notes of shorter duration (e.g. the *division* of four crotchets into sixteen semiquavers). In the transcription of the musical examples, the treble clef has been employed throughout, and minims have been substituted for semibreves, crotchets for minims, quavers for crotchets, &c., in order to facilitate reading and to give a clear impression of the pace of each dance at first sight. At the present time many people inevitably associate white notes with slow tempo; in the sixteenth century the minim was a relatively quick beat, and was used for very much the same purpose as we now use the crotchet.

Bar lines, which were by no means in universal employment in the sixteenth century, have been inserted at regular intervals, to mark off what Arbeau calls the *mesures* or metrical feet of the tune, in much the same way as the schoolboy is taught to scan his Virgil or his Ovid by barring the lines foot by foot.

PETER WARLOCK.

DIALOGUE

CONCERNING THE DANCE

AND THE PRACTICE OF DANCING

By THOINOT ARBEAU, *Residing at Langres*

Capriol. I come to greet you, M. Arbeau. You do not remember me, for it is six or seven years since I departed from this town of Langres to go to Paris, and from there to Orleans. I am an old pupil of yours whom you taught computation.

Arbeau. Certainly at first sight I did not recognise you for you have grown vastly since then. I hope you have likewise broadened your mind by virtue and knowledge. What do you think of the study of law ? At one time, I myself studied it.

Capriol. I find that it is a beautiful art, and one very necessary to the ordering of public affairs, but I regret that when at Orleans I neglected to learn the art of good manners which so many scholars acquire at the same time as their serious studies ; because, on my return, I found myself in a society in which I was forced to remain dumb, unable to speak or to move, and regarded as little more than a block of wood.

Arbeau. But you derived consolation in that the learned doctors excused this failing while mindful of the learning you had acquired.

Capriol. That is so, but I should have liked to acquire the art of dancing in the leisure hours between my studies ; it is an accomplishment that would have made my company agreeable to everyone.

Arbeau. That will be an easy thing to acquire by the reading of French books to sharpen your wit, and by the practice of sword-play, dancing and tennis, so as to be a pleasant companion for both ladies and gentlemen.

Capriol. I took a lively pleasure in sword-play and tennis which made me a good comrade for young men. But I know nothing of dancing and could not please the young ladies, on whom, it seems to me, the whole reputation of an eligible young man depends.

Arbeau. You have taken the proper view, because it is only natural that the male and female should seek each other, and nothing more disposes a man to acts of courtesy, honour and generosity than love ; and, if you desire to marry, you should know that a mistress is won by the pleasant disposition and grace with which one is observed to dance, for ladies do not like to be present at sword-play and tennis, for fear of a snapped blade or a blow from a tennis ball which might cause them hurt. You remember Virgil's lines telling of Turnus and his mistress, the beautiful Lavinia, daughter of King Latinus :—

> Illum turbat amor, figitque in virgine vultus :
> Ardet in arma magis, &c.[1]

There is more even in it than this, for dancing is practised to make manifest whether lovers are in good health and sound in all their limbs, after which it is permitted to them to kiss their mistresses, whereby they may perceive if either has an unpleasant breath or exhales a disagreeable odour as that of bad meat : so that, in addition to divers other merits attendant on dancing, it has become essential for the well-being of society.

Capriol. I have sometimes pondered on what you have just remarked. It is not without reason that games and dancing have formed part of the life of nations, but it has vexed me that dancing has been decried, even found paltry and considered as an effeminate exercise unworthy of the gravity of man. I have read that Cicero reproached the consul Gabinius for having danced. Tiberius expelled dancers from Rome. Domitian dismissed from the Senate any member who had danced. Alfonso, King of Arragon,

[1] Him love disturbeth much, and on the mayde his eyes he stayes,
And burnes to battell more.

reproved the Gauls because he saw them take delight in dancing. The holy prophet Moses was filled with wrath to see the children of Israel dance.

Arbeau. For one who has spoken ill of dances, there are an infinity of others who have praised and esteemed them. The holy and royal prophet David danced before the Ark of the Lord. And as for the holy prophet Moses, he was not angered to witness dancing, but grieved because it was performed round a Golden Calf, which was idolatry. As for Cicero, he had swollen veins and limbs and traduced that which he could not perform himself, saying that he did not like to see people dance who were fasting. Appius Claudius, after a victory, approved dances. Indians worship the sun with dances. And those who have voyaged to newly discovered lands report that the savages dance when the sun appears on the horizon. Socrates learned dancing from Aspasia. The *Salii*, the very noble priests of Mars danced at their sacrifices. The Corybants in Phrygia, the Lacedæmonians and the Cretans danced as they went against their foes. Vulcan engraved a dance on a shield as a very beautiful object for the eye. Museus and Orpheus desired that the hymns they had composed in honour of the gods should be sung to the accompaniment of dances. Bacchus conquered the Indies with three kinds of dances. In the primitive church there was a custom, which has endured until our own times, to sing the hymns of our faith while dancing, and this may still be observed in some places. Castor and Pollux taught the Carians to dance. Neoptolemus, the son of Achilles, taught the Cretans a dance called the *Pyrrhic* [1] to aid them in battle. Epaminondas employed dances very adroitly in the shock of battle, so that all could march as one against the enemy. Xenophon declared that dances and masquerades were devised to welcome the captains of Cyrus. Kings and princes have commanded the performances of dances and masquerades to divert, acclaim and give joyous greetings to foreign lords. We hold such rejoicings in honour of wedding-days and as part of the solemnities associated with our religious festivals, despite the reformers

[1] Plato states that the Pyrrhic dance " imitates the modes of avoiding blows and darts by dropping, or giving way, or springing aside, or rising up, or falling down ; also the opposite postures, which are those of action, as, for example, the imitation of archery and the hurling of javelins, and of all sorts of blows " (*Leg.*, vii., 815, Jowett's translation).

who abhor such practices; but they deserve to be fed on a piece of goat's flesh put without bacon into a pasty.

Capriol. You fill me with a longing to learn to dance and make me regret that I did not apply myself to it in my moments of leisure, for one can take honest pleasure without indulging in lewdness or evil practices. I recall that the poet places dancers among the happiest of beings, saying in the sixth book of the Aeneid :

Pars pedibus plaudunt choreas et carmina dicunt.[1]

Arbeau. You could quote further, that Our Lord (in the eleventh chapter of St. Matthew and the seventh of St. Luke) reproved the Pharisees for being obstinate and ill-disposed:

We have piped unto you and ye have not danced.

You must do as Demetrius did who, having traduced dances, confessed after he had witnessed a masquerade representing the mating of Mars with Venus, that never in the whole world had he seen anything so beautiful. In a little while you can make good this deficiency, since you are a musician and dancing is dependent on music, which is one of the seven liberal arts.

Capriol. I pray you then, M. Arbeau, teach me something of it, since I know well that you are a musician and that in your youth you earned the reputation of being a good dancer and very dexterous at a thousand gallantries.

Arbeau. The word dance comes from *danser*, which in Latin is called *saltare*. Dancing, so to speak, is to jump, to hop, to prance, to sway, to tread, to tip-toe, and to move the feet, hands and body in certain rhythms, measures and movements consisting of jumps, bendings of the body, straddlings, limpings, bendings of the knees, risings on tip-toe, throwings-forward of the feet, changes and other movements which Athenæus,[2] Celius, Scaliger and others have mentioned. In different times masks were worn to heighten the gestures of the personage represented. Lucian has written a treatise[3]

[1] Some frisking shake their feete, and measures tread and rimes they sowne.

[2] A learned Greek grammarian who flourished about A.D. 200. He wrote a miscellany called the *Banquet of the Learned,* which is very valuable for its information regarding Greek letters and science, and is set forth in the form of conversations of learned guests at a prolonged feast.

[3] Περὶ ὀρχήσεως, *De Saltatione*, a disputation between Lucian and Crates, a stoic philosopher, concerning dancing. Lucian was a warm

concerning it, where you can see at greater length what he maintained. Julius Pollux has likewise written an ample chapter upon this matter.

Capriol. I believe I have at some time read these authors and others like them, and if my memory serves me, they recount three kinds of dances; one grave, called the *Emmeleia;* one, gay, which they name the *Cordax*, and one other, partaking of both gravity and gaiety, called the *Sikinnis*. They make mention also of the dance called the *Pyrrhic* and many other kinds, as I recall that they mention divers masquerades, even one which they call the *Trichoria*, formed of three choirs composed respectively of greybeards, youths and little children, who sing: "We have been, we are and we shall be." I have some slight knowledge of these, but I wish to learn what steps and movements they used; please teach them to me.

Arbeau. Antoine d'Arena, a native of Provence, has set down in macaronic verses what you ask.

Capriol. In the verses you speak of, he has written only of the movements that must be made in *Branles* and *Basses Danses*, and the precepts that the dancers should observe, but the setting down in verse has made the meaning obscure, therefore I pray you enlighten me more concerning them.

Arbeau. Regarding ancient dances, I can say only that either the passing of time or the idleness of man, or the difficulty of describing them, has resulted in their being lost. So you need not trouble yourself about them, as such manners of dancing are no longer in fashion; even those that we have seen in the time of our fathers are no longer the dances of the present time, which is ever the case since men are such lovers of novelty. It is true that we can compare the *Emmeleia* to our *Pavanes* and *Basses-Danses*, the *Cordax* to *Gaillardes*, *Tordions*, *Voltes*, *Courantes*, *Gavottes*, *Branles de Champagne* and *de Bourgogne*, *Branles Gais* and *Branles Coupés;* the *Sikinnis* to *Branles Doubles* and *Branles Simples;* and the *Pyrrhic* to the dance we call *Bouffons* or *Mattachins*.

Capriol. I perceive then that those who come after us will

admirer of pantomimic dancing, to which he here gives the advantage over tragedy. A translation of this work will be found in *The Works of Lucian of Samosata* (trs. by H. W. Fowler and F. G. Fowler, 4 vols., 1905), Vol. 2, p. 238: *Of Pantomime*.

be ignorant of all these new dances you have just named, for the same reason that we have no knowledge of those of former times.

Arbeau. That is my belief.

Capriol. It is surely in your power, M. Arbeau, to repair this ? Set down in writing how I can achieve this polite art and as you write you will seem to be surrounded by the friends of your youth and to practice both mental and bodily exercise, for it will be difficult for you to abstain from moving your limbs in order to teach me the movements necessary to these dances. Certain it is that your method of writing is such that in your absence a pupil, studying your counsels and precepts in the seclusion of his chamber, could perform the movements. And first, I pray you, tell me in what esteem dancing is held by the majority of honourable men.

Arbeau. Dancing or saltation is an art both pleasing and profitable which confers and preserves health, is adapted for the youthful, agreeable to the aged and very suitable for all, so far as it is employed in fit place and season, without vicious abuse. I say in place and season, because it would be harmful to those who devoted themselves over zealously to it. You know what Ecclesiasticus says :

Cum muliere saltatrice non sis assiduus.[1]

The children of the Roman senators, on leaving school, went to learn to dance. Homer declares that dancing should be a part and an after-entertainment of banquets, so that none could boast of having given a brave feast if he had not joined dancing to it, which, if masquerades be added, becomes like a body endowed with a lively mind. When tragedies, comedies and pastorals were enacted in the ancient theatres, dances and gestures were not forgotten and that part of the theatre given up to this purpose was called the *Orchestra*, which, in our tongue, we may call the *Dançoir*.

Capriol. Since dancing is an art, it depends upon one of the seven liberal arts.

Arbeau. I have already told you that dancing depends on music because, without the virtue of rhythm, dancing would be meaningless and confused, so much so that it is necessary that the gestures of the limbs should keep time with the

[1] Use not much the company of a woman that is a dancer.

musical instruments and not the foot speak of one thing and the music of another. But practically all the *savants* hold that dancing is a kind of dumb rhetoric by which the orator, without speaking a single word, can, by virtue of his movements, make the spectators understand that he is gay, worthy to be praised, loved and adored. Is it not your opinion that dancing is a manner of speech, expressed in terms of the movements of the dancer's feet ? Does he not say tacitly to his mistress (who remarks the modesty and grace of his dancing) : " Dost thou not love me ? Dost thou not desire me ? " And when masquerades are added she has it in her power to move her lover sometimes to anger, sometimes to pity and commiseration ; sometimes to hatred, sometimes to ove. As we read of the daughter of Herodias who obtained what she demanded of King Herod Antipas after she had danced at the splendid banquet given by him on his birthday to the princes of his realm. So, too, with Roscius,[1] who proved to Cicero that he devised his gestures and mime in such a wise that, in the opinion of the arbiters, he moved the spectators as much as Cicero had been able to do by the eloquence of his orations, or even more.

Capriol. Roscius was an actor, and it seems to me that our laws brand such men as infamous.

Arbeau. Roscius was held and reputed (by the members of the Senate and by all the Romans who generally went to the theatre to observe him) a very honest and able man : so much so, that when it was desired to speak of a perfect artist, it was said that he was a Roscius in his art. Cicero pleaded for him in a suit he had against Fannius, and won his cause by the favour of the whole of the Senate, who loved, esteemed and honoured him. Those, indeed, who seek to gain wealth and admit indifferently any person to witness their plays and buffooneries are accounted infamous ; but the law has never included among these, men who perform simply for their own pleasure, and to afford diversion and entertainment to kings, princes, noble lords, the inhabitants of a town, or some particular company, by the playing of tragedies, comedies and pastorals represented with the face uncovered, or by dances to music with fine and graceful costumes to show their gaiety. And thus the Emperor has maintained in

[1] Q. Roscius, the most celebrated comic actor at Rome. For particulars of his career, *vide* William Smith, Dictionary of Greek and Roman Biography and Mythology (3 vols., 1849), Vol. III., p. 663.

the eleventh section of the Code, in the chapter on Public Games.

Capriol. I firmly believe that it should be understood thus. Do not delay any longer to grant my request nor keep me in expectation as to how the movements of the dances are performed, that I may practise myself in them, so as to avoid the reproach of having a pig's heart and an ass's head, as Lucian said to Crates.

Arbeau. Lucian did not address this reproof to those who did not wish to dance, or to those who desired to dance but could not acquire the art, but he attacked those who wished to censure and abolish dancing as an immoral practice, not considering that there are two kinds of dances, one of which is employed in war for the defence of the State, the other for amusement. The last has the virtue of attracting hearts to one another and inducing love, and is a preparation and a means (as I have told you already) to ascertain if persons be deformed by gout or wens on the legs, and if they be well favoured and modest. Do we not read that Cleisthenes,[1] having seen Hippocleides [2] dance and swagger shamelessly, refused him his daughter in marriage, saying that he had danced away his wedding ?

Capriol. Thanks be to God, I have none of these infirmities, and I have only a sister twelve years old to whom I shall expound all that you teach me.

Arbeau. Galen declares, in his book on the regimen of health, that all things have a natural desire for movement and that everyone should practise gentle and temperate motions such as dancing. The Ionians devised dances for this purpose, and for this reason dancing is of great value to the health, even to young girls who are given up to sedentary occupations and kept to their knitting, embroidery and stitchery so that they are subject to several ill humours, and have need to expel them by some moderate exercise.

Capriol. Dancing is a very fitting exercise for them,

[1] Son of Aristonymus and tyrant of Sicyon.

[2] An Athenian, son of Tisander. He was distinguished for his wealth and beauty of person. He came to the court of Cleisthenes as a suitor for his daughter Agarista, but failed through disgusting his host on the day appointed for the decision by a display of tumbler's tricks. Cleisthenes reproved him by saying : " You have danced away your marriage," to which he made the discourteous answer : " Hippocleides does not care."

since they are not free to take walks and to go here, there and everywhere about the towns as we can do without reproof, so that we do not need to practise dancing as much as they do ; nevertheless, I am very desirous of acquiring that art, at once so ancient, honourable and profitable.

Arbeau. To please you, I will tell you what I know of it, but, at my age of sixty-nine, it ill becomes me to indulge in this art. Let us speak first, then, of the warlike dances ; then we will treat of those that are for recreation. The instruments used for war dances are trumpets, bugles, horns and cornets ; flutes, fifes, pipes, drums and others similar to the last-named.

The Persian drum (which some Germans use, carrying it at the saddle-bow) consists of a hollow, leather hemisphere, the mouth closed with stout parchment, about two feet and a half in diameter. It makes a noise like thunder when the skin is struck with sticks.

The drum used by the French, familiar enough to everyone, is a hollow wooden cylinder about two feet and a half in length, closed at each end with parchment skins fixed with two bands, about two feet and a half in diameter, and bound with cords so that they are as tight as possible ; and this drum

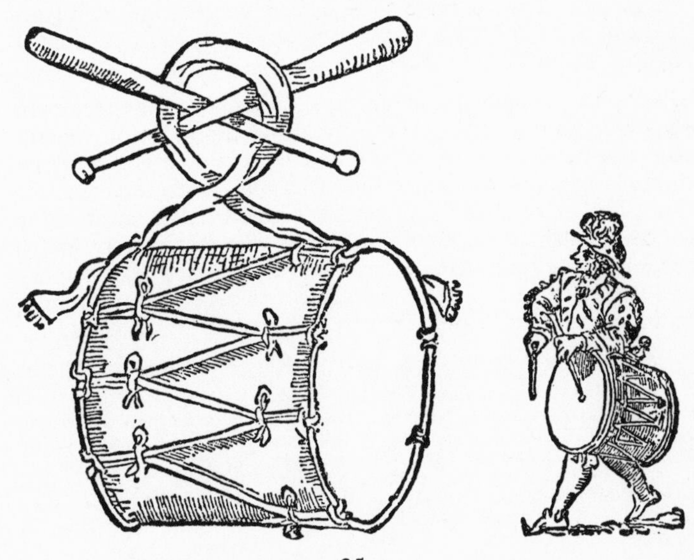

makes (as you have heard many times) a great noise when the said skins are beaten with the two sticks which the drummer holds in his hands. Everyone knows their appearance; all the same I will place a picture here since we are concerned with them.

Capriol. You have placed little straps and buckles at each crossing of the drum braces.

Arbeau. This is to tighten the skins when it is desired to beat the drum; the said buckles are then slid as near as possible to the middle, and when you wish to slacken them, the braces are loosened by approaching the said buckles towards the bands and edges. I do not know if the children of Israel used drums with one head as the Romans did at the sacrifice of the Mother of the Gods; but the fifteenth chapter of Exodus declares that Miriam, the sister of Moses and Aaron, was an excellent player of the drum. Virgil, in the sixth book of the Aeneid, speaking of Misenus, at first trumpeter to Hector and after to Aeneas, says these words:

> [1] Quo non præstantior alter
> Aere ciere viros, martemque accendere cantu,

and a little further on,

> [2] Et lituo pugnas insignis obibat, et hasta.

The sound of all these instruments serves as a sign and a signal to the soldiers to change quarters, advance, or retire: and, in an encounter with the enemy, to give them stout hearts, boldness and courage to attack the foe and to defend themselves in a manly and vigorous manner. Now, were it not for these, the men would march confusedly and without order which would cause them to be in danger of being overthrown and defeated; that is why our French soldiers are commanded to make the ranks and squads march to certain rhythms.

Capriol. How is that?

Arbeau. You are a musician and know well the nature of measures and rhythms; some are duple,[3] others triple,[4] and these two kinds of time may be divided further into slow, moderate and quick.

[1] Whose nobler never was
In kindling men with noise, and fighting fields to cheer with brass.

[2] With trompet bold and speare he corage gave in battaill throng.

[3] *E.g.*, $\frac{2}{4}$ or common time, in modern parlance.

[4] *E.g.*, $\frac{3}{4}$ or $\frac{3}{2}$ as the case may be.

Capriol. That is true.

Arbeau. You will admit that if three men are walking together and each of them wishes to go at a different rate according to the three kinds of time, they will not be in step, because all three must march as one, whether quickly, slowly or at a moderate rate of speed.

Capriol. There is not the slightest doubt about it.

Arbeau. That is why, in a military march, the French have employed a drum to beat the rhythm according to which the soldiers must march, all the more so because the majority of them are no better exercised in this than in any other branches of the military art. And for that reason I shall not delay in writing out the different methods.

A drum-rhythm contains eight crotchets, of which the first five are beaten and struck, that is to say, the first four with one tap of the stick only, the fifth with the two sticks together; and the other three beats are silent and are not struck.

Tan tan tan tan tan

In the time occupied by these five crotchets and the three rests the soldier takes a pace, that is to say, he strides forward so that, on the first note, he brings his left foot into position, and during the other three notes raises the right foot to bring it into position on the fifth note; and, during the three rests, which are of equal duration to three notes, he again raises his left foot to recommence another pace as before. Consequently, if the distance travelled be such that the drum-rhythm is repeated two thousand five hundred times, the soldier marches the length of a league.

Capriol. Why do you step off with the left foot first?

Arbeau. Because most men are right-footed, and, as the left foot is the weaker, if it should chance to hesitate for any reason, the right foot would immediately be ready to support it.

Capriol. It seems to me that what is called a pace, in Latin *passus*, is said to be the length of the two arms extended and not that of the two feet.

Arbeau. Look carefully and ascertain, by measuring it, if the pace of the two feet be not the same length as the two arms extended, which geometricians consider to be five feet.

Capriol. Have you not reckoned falsely in saying that to march a league the drum-rhythm must be repeated two thousand five hundred times, because a league contains only two thousand paces, which makes two thousand drum-rhythms, allowing, as you say, one pace to each repetition of the drum-rhythm ?

Arbeau. Certainly a single pace is equal to five feet and two thousand paces to a league, but when many paces, one after the other, are made in time with the drum, each contains four feet only, all the more so since the foot that completes the first step is placed ready to begin the second, and so on from pace to pace, so that the said paces each contain but four feet, and thus one league requires two thousand five hundred paces, which makes two thousand lengths each of five geometric feet.

Capriol. I quite understand it now.

Arbeau. Another matter you must consider is that when the drum-rhythms are varied, they are rendered more pleasing. And for this reason the drummers sometimes dispose the five crotchets and the three rests as we have noted above, sometimes in place of one of the crotchets they put two quavers or four semi-quavers, as it pleases them; however, the fifth note must always be a crotchet, unless they wish to continue for two, three or more repetitions of the rhythm, for then the three rests do not occur except at the end.

Capriol. I understand this more or less, but I should like very much to have examples of these several varieties of rhythm.

Arbeau. The several varieties are obtained by different intermixtures of crotchets, quavers and semi-quavers.

Capriol. Let me see a tabulation of them.

Arbeau. You are well aware that a crotchet is equal to two quavers, and that a quaver is equal to two semi-quavers, hence, during the time of one crotchet, two quavers or four semi-quavers can be beaten and, to understand this better, let us call the sound of a crotchet, which is made with one tap of the stick, Tan or Plan. And let us call the sound of two quavers which are made with two taps of the sticks, Tĕrĕ, and the sound of four semi-quavers, made by four taps of the sticks, Frĕ. Then, let us combine these varieties one with another, and we shall find them very diversified. Here is a tabulation from which you will choose the kinds that please you most.

Tabulation containing every variety of drum-rhythm.

The first manner is composed of five Tan only, as has been noted elsewhere.

Tan tan tan tan tan

The other drum-rhythms are composed of a combination of Tan with Tĕrĕ, of Tan with Frĕ, and of the three together, Tan, Tĕrĕ and Frĕ.

And first is a combination of four Tan with one Tĕrĕ, which can be achieved in four ways.

Combination of three Tan and two Tĕrĕ.

Tan tan tĕrĕ tĕrĕ tan

Tan tĕrĕ tĕrĕ tan tan

Tan tĕrĕ tan tĕrĕ tan

Tĕrĕ tĕrĕ tan tan tan

Tĕrĕ tan tĕrĕ tan tan

Tĕrĕ tan tan tĕrĕ tan

Combination of two Tan and three Tĕrĕ.

Tan tĕrĕ tĕrĕ tĕrĕ tan

Tĕrĕ tan tĕrĕ tĕrĕ tan

Tĕre tĕrĕ tan tĕrĕ tan

Tĕrĕ tĕrĕ tĕrĕ tan tan

Another combination of four Tĕrĕ and one Tan, which cannot be arranged otherwise, because there must be a Tan at the end to mark the cadence.

Tĕrĕ tĕrĕ tĕrĕ tĕrĕ tan

Combination of four Tan and one Frĕ.

Combination of three Tan and two Frĕ, of which there are six kinds as follow.

Tan frĕ frĕ tan tan

Tan frĕ tan frĕ tan

Frĕ frĕ tan tan tan

Frĕ tan frĕ tan tan

Frĕ tan tan frĕ tan

Combination of two Tan and three Frĕ, of which there are four kinds.

Tan frĕ frĕ frĕ tan

Frĕ tan frĕ frĕ tan

Frĕ frĕ tan frĕ tan

Frĕ frĕ frĕ tan tan

Another drum-rhythm composed of four Frĕ and one Tan, which cannot be arranged otherwise.

Combination of three Tĕrĕ and one Frĕ, with the final Tan.

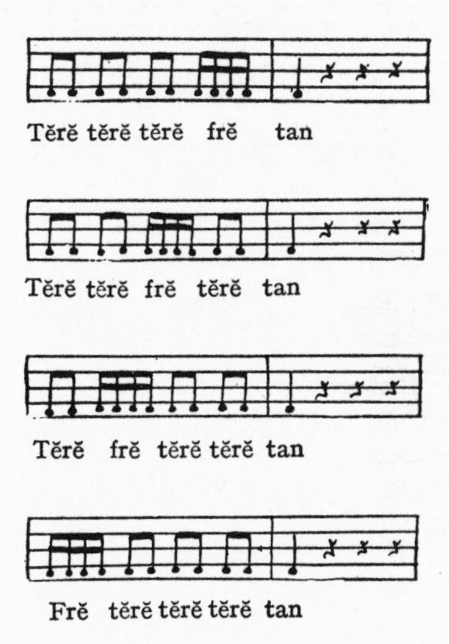

Capriol. I do not think that the drum is capable of any other rhythms than those you have set down above.

Arbeau. The setting down of them has wearied you perhaps, but there are still other varieties which I shall note, since I am unwilling to leave unfinished what I have begun.

Combination of two Tĕrĕ and two Frĕ with the final Tan.

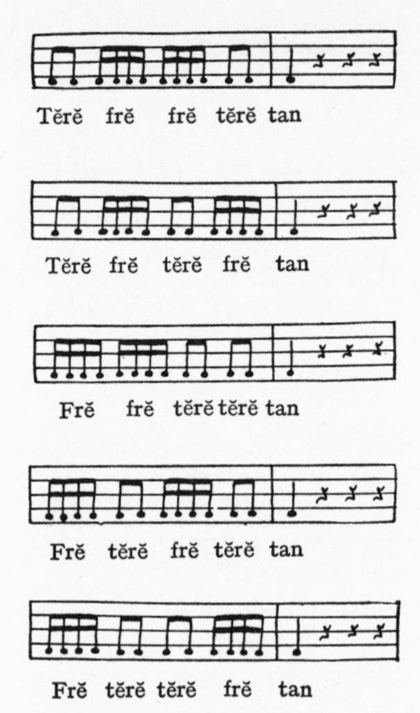

Combination of one Těrě and three Frě with the final Tan, which can be done in four ways, after which I will show you the other kinds.

Combination of three Tan, one Tĕrĕ and one Frĕ, which can be done in twelve ways, as follow.

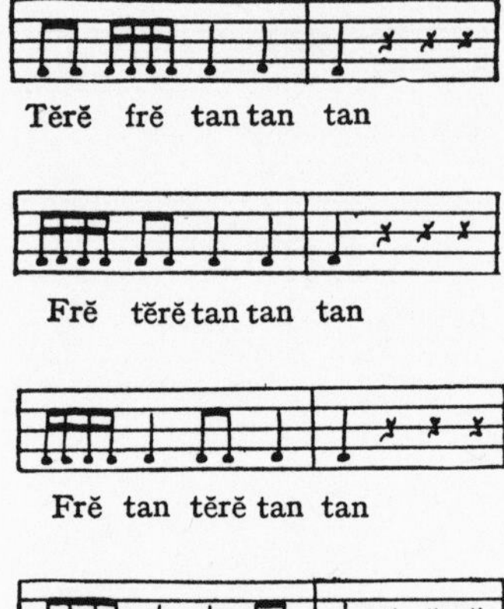

Combination of two Tan, two Těrě and one Frě, which can be done in twelve ways, as follow.

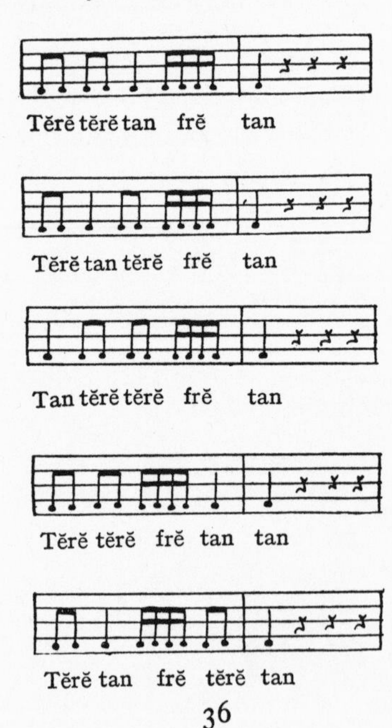

Tan tĕrĕ frĕ tĕrĕ tan

Tan frĕ tĕrĕ tĕrĕ tan

Tĕrĕ frĕ tĕrĕ tan tan

Tĕrĕ frĕ tan tĕrĕ tan

Frĕ tan tĕrĕ tĕrĕ tan

Frĕ tĕrĕ tan tĕrĕ tan

Frĕ tĕrĕ tĕrĕ tan tan

Combination of two Tan, one Tĕrĕ and two Frĕ, which can be done in eight ways, as follow.

Frĕ frĕ tĕrĕ tan tan

Frĕ frĕ tan tĕrĕ tan

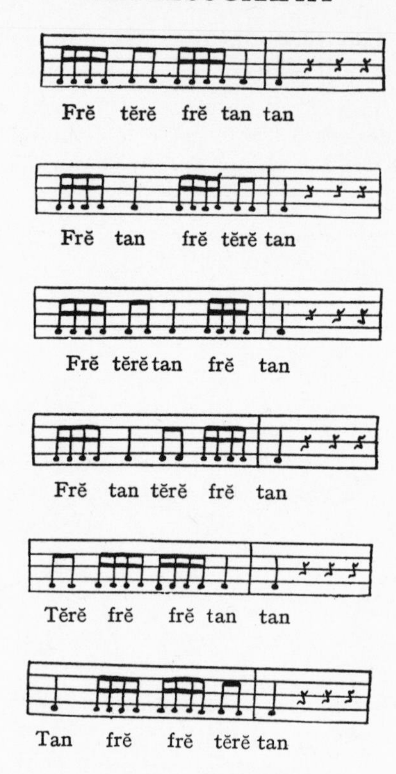

Among all the varieties set down above a drummer can choose those which appear to him to be the most pleasing and best sounding to the ear.

Capriol. Why are these rests written ? Why cannot the drummer use eight crotchets for each pace—four for the left foot and four for the right?

Arbeau. If the drummer did not make use of rests, the soldiers' steps would fall into confusion, because, as I have told you, the left foot must be put down on the first note and the right on the fifth ; and if all the eight notes were struck, a soldier could put down his feet on notes other than the first and the fifth. But this does not happen if you add rests and pauses, for, by their beating thus, he hears distinctly the first and the fifth notes.

Capriol. Can these rests in the drum-rhythms occur only after the fifth note ?

Arbeau. The Swiss drummers put a rest after the third note and three rests at the end, but it all amounts to the same, because the feet are always put down on the first and fifth notes.

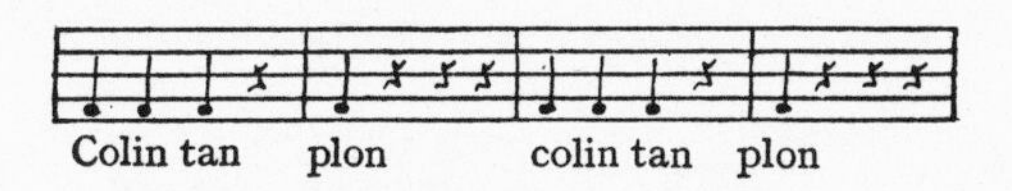

Capriol. This manner of marching to the sound of the drum must be very pleasing when strict time is kept.

Arbeau. It can be done otherwise than by the said duple time by putting only one rest after the five crotchet notes, and in this case the soldier puts down his left foot on the first note, then his right on the third note, then his left foot again on the fifth note. And in the bar which follows, he puts down his right foot on the first note, his left on the third note, and then his right foot again on the fifth note, continuing in this manner for the distance to be covered.

Capriol. According to this reckoning, each drum-rhythm accounts for a greater length of road than he could cover in his marching by paces.

Arbeau. That is certain. For the first drum-rhythm covers seven feet, and all the others following six feet only.

And, by this means, the soldier traverses a league in one thousand, six hundred and sixty-six drum-rhythms or thereabout. It would also be possible to beat the said five crotchets and one rest, and to march to them in triple time.

In the triple time the soldier puts down his left foot on the first note, and his right foot on the fourth note, and so on.

Capriol. This triple time is very pleasing; the paces taken are similar to those in duple time, and thus there is only one rest and pause.

Arbeau. When the warriors approach the enemy, they march in closer formation and must very carefully observe their steps, as I have told you, by putting down the left foot on the first note.

Capriol. But if the soldier puts down his right foot on the said first note, does not that amount to the same thing?

Arbeau. Not exactly, because, presupposing the majority of soldiers are right-footed, they march with the left foot first, so that if any of them began with the right and finished with the left, their shoulders would knock one against the other when they closed up, and they would hinder one another by thrusting forward the shoulder on the side of the foot put down. If, therefore, a soldier began with the left foot, his shoulder would be inclined to the left, and the shoulder of the one who began with the right foot would be inclined to the right, and they would knock against each other. This does not occur if all march in step, for the shoulders all incline first to one side and then to the other without hindering or knocking into each other, which you can easily ascertain by walking with someone. That is why the drummer beats a succession of many repetitions of the drum-rhythm together, so that if there be any confusion due to an alteration of the march, the soldiers could easily set it right and begin again quite easily on the left foot after they have heard the pause or the three rests. And this is of the greatest assistance in making evolutions.

Capriol. What are evolutions?

Arbeau. It is not our intention here to treat of the military art; if you wish to know the meaning of evolution, consult the book which Aelian[1] dedicated to the Emperor Hadrian. All I shall tell you is that, in addition to the marches, saltations and war dances noted above, the drummer employs a succession of lighter and quicker strokes composed of quavers, combining with them loud blows of the sticks, which resemble the discharge of many arquebuses, and this is done when the soldiers approach near to the enemy; and when they wish to join battle they close up one against the other, as if they were one mass, lowering their pikes and bills and making of them a strong and solid rampart difficult to move or break asunder.

[1] Ælianus Tacticus, who flourished about 100 A.D. He wrote a treatise on Greek tactics dedicated to the Emperor Hadrian. It has been translated into English by Captain John Bingham in 1616, and by Lord Dillon in 1814.

The drummer all the while beats two quavers in a quick duple rhythm derived from the metrical foot which poets call the Pyrrhic,[1] and the soldiers advance, keeping the left foot forward all the while and putting it down on the first note of the Pyrrhic. And on the second note of the Pyrrhic, they place the right foot behind and near to the said left foot, so as to form a buttress. And leaping and dancing thus, they commence the fight, as if the drum wished to say:

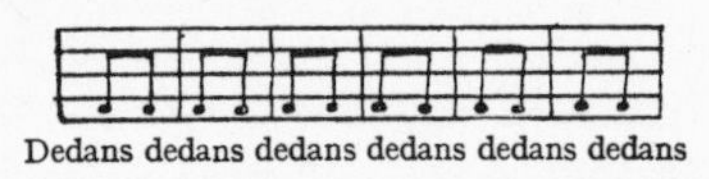

Capriol. It seems to me that I now ought to march and dance very well in the military fashion according to the strokes and rhythms of the drum. But why is the drummer accompanied by one or two fifers ?

Arbeau. What we call the fife is a little transverse flute with six holes, which the Germans and Swiss use, and as its bore is very narrow, only the width of a pistol bullet, it gives a shrill sound. Some use, in place of the fife, the flageolet or small flute called a pipe,[2] which, according to its size, has a greater or lesser number of holes. The best have four holes in front and two behind, and their sound is very piercing; they might be called small *tibiæ*, because they were first made of the thigh and shin bones of cranes. The players of the said drums and fifes are called after the names of their instruments, and we say of two soldiers that one is the drummer and the other the fifer of some captain.

Capriol. Is there a particular manner of playing the fife or pipe ?

Arbeau. Those who play them play as they please, and it is sufficient for them to keep time with the sound of the drum. All the same, we read that the Phrygian mode, which musicians call the third mode, incites naturally to anger, and that the Lydians used it when going to war. History relates that when Timotheus[3] made use of it, playing on his *tibia*, Alexander the Great immediately rose up like a madman

[1] *ποὺς πυρρίχιος*. A foot consisting of two short syllables which was used in the *πυρρίχη* or war-song.

[2] *Arigot.*

[3] Timotheus of Miletus (circa 446–357 B.C.), a Greek dithyrambic poet and musician.

burning for a fight. Bacchus, that great captain named Dionysus, taught his soldiers, surrounded by the camp-women, to dance and make warlike marches to the sound of the drum and the Phrygian *tibia*, and by this means subjugated the Indians, who marched in disorderly masses with cries and yells, and consequently were disturbed and easily put to flight and vanquished.

Capriol. Give me a tabulation of the music for the fife or pipe as you have of that for the drum.

Arbeau. I have told you that the music of the fife or pipe is improvised at the player's pleasure. All the same, I will give you here a little extract that I have obtained from M. Isaac Huguet, the organist. Its compass, on his spinet, extends from middle C, or the B below it, as far as E (a tenth above). To imitate the drum the spinet-player, by way of making a bass, puts his left thumb on C (octave below middle C), his little finger on the C an octave below it, and strikes them alternately, the lower C on the first beat, and the upper C on the fifth, keeping his first finger on the G, which makes a perfect fifth with the said lower C and a fourth with the upper.

Capriol. It seems to me, saving your correction, that by the rules of music this fourth ought not to be used as a bass.

Arbeau. You are quite right, in so far as vocal music in four parts is concerned, but in the present case we are concerned with the sound of the drum, which serves as a bass, and because it has no definite pitch or tone it accords with everything as I have told you, and it matters not that the spinet should represent it by these harmonious discords. But before I give you the example you must remember that there are two ways of playing the flute. In the former the player's tongue goes té té té, or tĕrĕ tĕrĕ tĕrĕ ; and in the latter, relé relé relé. I warn you of this because the example I wish to write out for you must be played té té té and not rolled.

Capriol. Why should you play té té té rather than the roll ?

Arbeau. Because the sound produced by the té té té is sharper and rougher and consequently more warlike than the roll.

Tabulation for the fife or arigot, in the third mode.

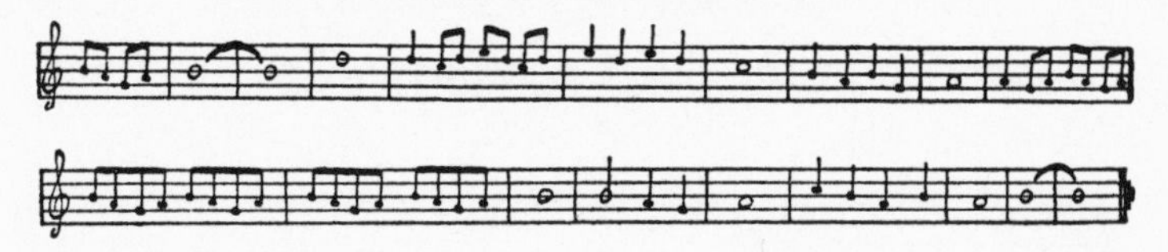

Capriol. I am very pleased to have this example. I have a little pipe and I shall try to play on it the air you have given me.

Arbeau. You can amplify this music at your pleasure and fantasy. And if, peradventure, you suppose the drum is beaten in a triple rhythm which consists of five crotchets and a rest [1] you can make use of the above music by subtracting two crotchets from each bar, sometimes at the end of the phrase, sometimes at the beginning, sometimes in the middle, so that the continuity should not be broken.

Capriol. Those who understand music can easily play it.

Arbeau. I wish to give you one example in triple time which you can use without having the trouble of subtracting the above-named notes if you do not wish to do so : this you can also amplify as much as you like.

Capriol. Since it pleases you to take this trouble you will greatly oblige me.

Tabulation for playing the fife or arigot in triple time.

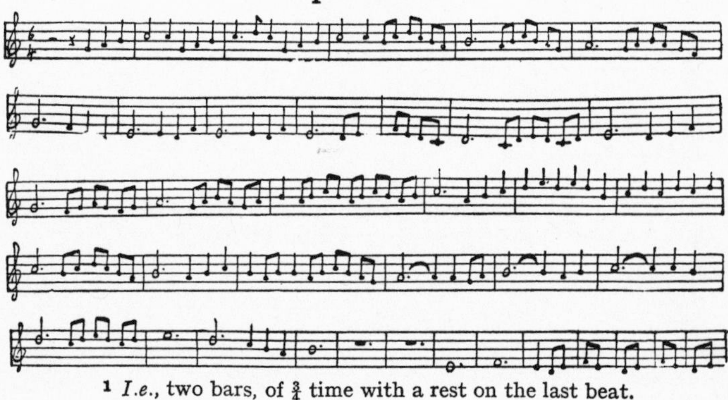

[1] *I.e.*, two bars, of $\frac{3}{4}$ time with a rest on the last beat.

Capriol. I have no desire to go to war ; all the same, these rules that you have given me concerning war-like dances may be of use to me when we practise military evolutions in the town of Langres. But, for the moment, let us say no more about this ; now tell me about dances for pleasure.

Arbeau. First, I must inform you that in the likeness of the drum of which we have spoken above, a little one has been fashioned called the tabor, or small hand drum, about two feet long and a foot in diameter, which Isidorus calls a Half-Symphony, on the skin extremities of which twisted threads are placed, while on the big drum a double cord is placed across one of the skins only.

Capriol. What is the purpose of these twisted threads ?

Arbeau. It is due to them that when the tabor is struck with a little stick or with the fingers, its sound is strident and vibrating.

Capriol. Symphony means harmony and not a tabor.

Arbeau. True, this Greek word Symphony means harmony and from this word musicians are called Symphonists. But it is not inappropriate that the tabor has received the name of Symphony which Isidorus calls a Half-Symphony, because it is usually accompanied by one or more musical instruments with which it accords, serving them as a Bass or Diapason to all harmonies ; similarly it is employed with the instrument called Chorus to give praise to God in rejoicing, which the Royal Prophet speaks of when he says: *Laudate Dominum in tympano et choro*. In the fifteenth chapter of St. Luke the elder son of the father of a family was indignant when he learned that, for the welcoming of his brother, they were making good cheer with the fatted calf to the accompaniment of the Symphony and the Chorus. Daniel, in his third chapter, says that Nebuchadnezzar proclaimed that every subject should worship his image as soon as they heard the flute, hautboy, sackbut, harp, psaltery, symphony, and other kinds of music being played.

Capriol. I had interpreted this word Chorus as meaning a company of dancers.

Arbeau. I have seen a representation of the said instrument Chorus in a book where all manner of instruments were described, and it was placed with the Symphony or tabor, as nowadays this is joined to the flute or large *tibia*. The Basques and Béarnais use another kind of tabor [1] which they hold suspended from the left hand, playing it with the fingers of the right. The wood is hollow for half a foot only and the skins a foot in diameter, and it is surrounded with little bells and pieces of copper making an agreeable sound and not a hideous din like the large drums fitted with little bells, described by Suidas, which the Indians use in their battles. As for our tabor we do not put any bells on it at all, and generally accompany it with a long flute or large *tibia*. And with the said flute the musician plays all the airs which seem good to him, holding it with the left hand which supports the tabor.

Capriol. Is it possible that he could play an air with the left hand alone? I cannot credit it, because I find it difficult enough to find the different notes with both hands on a flute with nine holes, and thus it seems to me impossible to hold and play it with the same hand.

Arbeau. The top end is held in the player's mouth and the lower end rests between the third and fourth fingers, and, that it may not slip through the player's hand, there is a little cord at the end of the flute by which the third finger

[1] The French word translated *tabor* is *tambourin* throughout the text. But the particular kind of tabor here mentioned is what we should now call a *tambourine*.

holds and supports it. It has three holes only, two in front and one behind, and it is admirably devised because with the first and second fingers touching the two holes in front, and with the thumb touching the hole behind, all the notes of the scale are easily produced.

Capriol. This, then, is a secret which I would willingly learn by the way, and then I will pray you to continue your remarks.

Arbeau. You must know that pipes which are tall and long and have a narrow bore, like the flute in question, will easily and naturally overblow a fifth. And if they are blown harder still, they will sound the octave. So that when the long flute is blown softly and all the holes are stopped, suppose it sounds G, then, if the first hole closed by the middle finger be opened, it will sound the A above it ; if, further, the second hole, closed by the first finger, be opened, it will sound B ; and if the third hole, which is behind and closed by the thumb, be opened, it will sound C. After that, all of the holes being quite closed, by blowing a little harder it jumps to the fifth above and sounds D. With the same breath, if the middle finger be raised it will sound E, and now raising the first finger it will sound F. This accomplished, by raising the thumb it will sound G, and continuing thus and raising the fingers, and making the blast as strong as needed, many different notes are obtained.

Capriol. You make this upper octave G by raising the thumb ; then, by closing all the holes, it should sound the A above it.

Arbeau. If all the holes be closed it sounds the octave also, on account of the natural disposition of this type of flute which, when all the holes are closed, jumps to the fifth and then to the octave.

Capriol. As it is said in Terence that the comedy of *Andria* was played to the accompaniment of the unequal *tibiæ* of Claudius, must not these be the flutes of which you have spoken ?

Arbeau. Certainly, I believe so, for one finds in antique sculpture that the same person played two flutes together, of which one was larger and sounded deeper, the other shorter and sounded shriller. The larger was held in the left hand and the shorter in the right. And, in my opinion, they were held thus for the better and more effective rendering of the cadences by the said right hand. Coming from Saint Claud's Mount, which Ptolemy calls Mount Ivras, I recollect having seen a double flute played, one pipe of which was cut shorter, equal to a third of the larger, and the person who played them with both hands made their sounds blend harmoniously.

Capriol. Valerius Maximus [1] in the chapter on ancient institutions speaks of the college of *tibia* players.

Arbeau. This college was like the bands of musicians found in towns; they played on a variety of *tibiæ*, some like those of which we have been speaking, others with nine holes, others again with reed tongues whose sound resembles, like our hautboys, that of trumpets, of which the poet Horace speaks thus :

> [2] Tibia non ut nunc oricalcho cincta, tubaeque
> Aemula.

Capriol. Truly hautboys greatly resemble trumpets and make a sufficiently pleasing harmony when the large ones, sounding the lower octave, are combined with the little hautboys which sound the higher.

Arbeau. These two are excellent for making a loud noise, such as is required for village *fêtes* and large assemblies, but, if it be combined with the flute, it drowns the sound of it. It may be well combined with the tabor, or with the large drum.

[1] A Roman historian of Tiberius's reign.

[2] The hau'boy, not as now with latten bound,
And rival with the trumpet for his sound.

Capriol. Can the large drum be used for recreative dances ?

Arbeau. Yes, certainly, especially with the said hautboys, which are noisy and screeching, and are blown with force.

Capriol. Let us return to the question of the tabor and the dance.

Arbeau. The tabor, accompanied by its long flute among other instruments, was employed in our fathers' time because a single musician could play them together in complete accord, thus avoiding the great expense of having many other players, such as violists and the like. Nowadays, the meanest workman must have hautboys and sackbuts at his wedding, when many kinds of recreative dances are performed.

Capriol. Tell me what these dances are, and how they are performed.

Arbeau. *Pavanes*, *Basses-Danses*, *Branles* and *Courantes* are danced. *Basses-Danses* have been out of fashion some forty or fifty years. But I foresee that wise and decorous matrons will restore them to favour as being a manner of dancing full of honour and modesty.

Capriol. How did our forefathers dance the *Basse-Danse ?*

Arbeau. There were two kinds of *Basses-Danses*, one common and regular, the other irregular. The former were fitted to regular, and the latter to irregular airs.

Capriol. What do you call common and regular airs ?

Arbeau. In such a case the musicians composed sixteen-bar airs which they repeated and thus there were thirty-two bars for the beginning; and for the middle part they put sixteen bars, and for the end sixteen bars repeated. Thus the common and regular *Basse-Danse* was composed of eighty bars in all. And if it happened that the air exceeded these eighty bars the *Basse-Danse* accompanying it was called irregular.

Capriol. What movements must be made during these bars?

Arbeau. You should know beforehand that the airs of the *Basses-Danses* are played in triple time and at each bar the tabor, to accord with the flute, beats triple time too.

In beating the eighty drum-rhythms with the little stick each of these contain one crotchet and four quavers, thus:—

And to each bar the dancer makes the movements of the feet and body according to the rules of the dance.

Capriol. How shall I perform these movements when I wish to dance a *Basse-Danse* [1]?

Arbeau. First, when you have entered the place where the company is gathered together for the dance, you will choose some modest damsel who pleases your fancy and, doffing your hat or bonnet with your left hand, offer her your right to lead her out to dance. She, having been well brought up, will offer you her left hand, rise and follow you. Then you will lead her in the sight of every one to the end of the room and instruct the musicians to play some *Basse-Danse*; for, otherwise, they might inadvertently play some other kind of dance. And when they begin to play, you will begin to dance. And observe that, in requesting a *Basse-Danse* of them, they will quite understand that you desire a regular and common one; however, if the air of some one particular song on which a *Basse-Danse* is founded be more pleasing to you than another, you could tell them how it begins.

[1] Literally *Low Dance.* Formerly, this term was applied to all dances executed *terre à terre* and without jumping, while a dance was called *haute* (high) if executed while jumping. *Cf.* G. Desrat, *Dictionnaire de la Danse,* 1895, p. 49.

Capriol. If the damsel refused me I should be overcome with shame.

Arbeau. A well-bred damsel will never refuse the man who does her the honour of asking her to dance ; and, if she did, she would be accounted foolish, for if she did not desire to dance she ought not to take her place among the others.

Capriol. I well believe it ; yet, the shame of the refusal would fall upon me.

Arbeau. If you are assured of the good graces of another damsel in the company, you should take her and leave the discourteous one alone, asking her pardon for having been so forward ; all the same, it is not every one who would bear it so patiently, yet it is better to speak fairly than with bitterness, and by doing so, you will acquire the reputation of being pleasant and good-natured, and throw back on the damsel the stigma of being proud and unworthy of the honour you paid her.

Capriol. Here we are then, standing at the end of the room ; the musicians begin to play a *Basse-Danse.* With what movements do we begin to dance ?

Arbeau. The first movement is the *revérénce,*[1] marked by a big **R** ; the second is the *branle,*[2] marked **b**. The third kind of movement, consisting of two *simples,*[3] is marked **ss**. The fourth is the *double* [4] marked **d**, the fifth is the *reprise,*[5] marked by a little **r**.

Capriol. Is that all that is necessary in dancing a common and regular *Basse-Danse ?*

Arbeau. There are no other kinds of movements in the *basse-danse* or in the *retour de la basse-danse,*[6] although these same ones are repeated several times.

Capriol. What do you mean by " *retour de la basse-danse ?* "

[1] Literally *bow.* The term may be rendered more completely as the lady's curtsey and the gentleman's bow.
[2] Literally *shake.*
[3] Literally *single.*
[4] Literally *double.*
[5] Literally *repetition.*
[6] Literally *return of the* basse-danse.

Arbeau. The complete *Basse-Danse* contains three parts. The first is called the *basse-danse*, the second the *retour de la basse-danse*, and the third and last the *tordion*. I have put a tabulation of it here in writing so that you can learn it by heart.

Tabulation of the movements for the *basse-danse.*

R b ss d r d r b ss ddd r d r b ss d r b c

Capriol. What is the meaning of the letter **c** which you have placed at the end ?

Arbeau. It signifies the *congé* [1] which must be taken of the damsel. You salute her, keeping hold of her hand to return her to the place where the dance was begun, so as to perform the second part or the *retour de la basse-danse.*

Tabulation of the movements for the *retour de la basse-danse.*

b d r b ss ddd r d r b c

This final letter **c** signifies *congé* like the other and there is no big **R** at all at the beginning of this *retour* because it is begun without making the *révérence*, which is not done again until after the *congé*, before beginning the *tordion*.

Capriol. Show me in detail the gestures and movements signified by these letters and tabulations.

Arbeau. The *révérence*, the first gesture and movement, occupies four drum-rhythms which accompany four bars of the air played by the flute. Antoine d'Arena, considering that all dances begin with the left foot, was of the opinion that the *révérence* ought to be made with the left. However, he seems to leave the matter in doubt at the end, saying thus :

> [2] Bragardi certant et adhuc sub judice lis est
> De quali gamba sit facienda salus.

As for myself, I hold with my master, under whom I formerly studied at Poitiers, that it should be done with the right foot.

[1] Literally *leave*.

[2] It is still a disputed point with which leg the first step (leap) should be taken.

In this manner one can turn the body and face toward the damsel and bestow upon her a gracious look.

Capriol. The *branle* succeeds the *révérence ;* how should this be performed ?

Arbeau. The *branle* is called *Congedium* by Arena, and I believe that it is so called because, to look at the dancer's gestures, it would seem that he desired to finish and take his *congé* of the damsel. Nevertheless, after the *branle*, he continues his steps and movements, as they are written in the tabulation. The *branle* is danced in the time of four drum-rhythms, which accompany four bars of the air played by the flute, by keeping the feet together and turning the body gently to the left for the first bar ; then to the right, glancing modestly at the onlookers, for the second ; then again to the left for the third ; and to the right for the fourth, gazing softly and discreetly at the damsel the while, with a sidelong glance.

Capriol. Two *simples* follow the *branle ;* how should they be done ?

Arbeau. For the first bar, you will take one step forward with the left foot. Then for the second, bring the right foot up against the left. Then, for the third, take one step forward with the right foot. And at the fourth bring the left foot against the right and thus the movement of the two *simples* [1] will be completed. And care must be taken that you do not take such long steps that it would seem as if you wished to measure the length of the room, since the damsel cannot in modesty take such long paces as you can. Arena and others of his school execute the *simple* with the same foot, marking the first bar by bringing the left to the side of the right, then advancing the left again. And in the same manner with the right foot. But I remember that my teacher at Poitiers improved this custom, saying that it was more decent to finish the two *simples* with the feet together than with one foot advanced.

Capriol. This reasoning seems sound to me and I shall follow your advice. But now let us speak of the *double*, how should this be performed ?

Arbeau. The *double* occupies four bars or four drum-rhythms for its execution. In the first bar, you must take one step forward with the left foot ; in the second the right must take one step forward ; in the third the left must be advanced again ; and in the fourth the right must be brought to the side of the left. Thus in four bars the *double* [2] will be completed. And if there are two *doubles*, the second is done contrariwise to the first, advancing the right foot, then the left, then the right again, and in the fourth bar the left must be brought to the side of the right. Thus in eight bars two *doubles* will have been performed. And to execute still a third *double*, the left foot must be advanced, then the right, then the left, finishing with the feet together as was done in the first. Thus the three *doubles* are completed in twelve bars or twelve drum-rhythms.

Capriol. I have still to learn how a *reprise* is executed.

Arbeau. This movement called the *reprise* generally precedes the *branle* and sometimes the *double ;* it occupies four bars or drum-rhythms like the other movements, and you

[1] The *simple* is merely a walking step and feet-together, or a *pas marché* followed by an *assemblé*.

[2] A *double* is simply three walking steps and feet-together, or three *pas marchés* executed with alternate feet and followed by an *assemblé*.

perform it by slightly shaking the knees, or the feet, or the toes only, as if your feet trembled. So that it is done with the toes of the right foot on the first bar, again with the same on the second, then with the toes of the left foot on the third, and with the right on the fourth. And in these four movements the *reprise* will be accomplished and the dancer ready to perform the *branle* or the movements which follow it.

Capriol. Supposing we call the four bars of the drum and flute a quaternion or tetradion, I find, in counting the characters which you have given me as a tabulation, that the *basse-danse* contains twenty quaternions; and the *retour de la basse-danse* twelve.

Arbeau. Your reckoning is correct. And after the *basse-danse* and the *retour de la basse-danse* you can begin to dance the *tordion*, which is in triple time like the *basse-danse*. But it is lighter and more animated.

Capriol. Is this *tordion* composed of the same movements as the *basse-danse* and its *retour*—that is to say, of *simples*, *doubles*, *reprises* and *branles ?*

Arbeau. It comprises another group of movements which is composed of certain positions of the feet and a cadence which I will explain to you more clearly when we speak of the *Gaillarde*, because the *tordion* is simply a *Gaillarde* danced keeping the feet close to the ground.

Capriol. Teach me the movements of this *Gaillarde*.

Arbeau. We shall consider it after we have spoken of the *Pavane*, which is usually danced prior to the *Basse-Danse*. The *Pavane* has not disappeared or passed out of fashion, nor do I think it ever will, though it is true that it is not favoured as it was in the past. Our musicians play it when a damsel of good family is taken to Holy Church to be married or when musicians head a procession of the chaplains, master and brethren of some notable guild.

Capriol. While awaiting your instruction in the *Gaillarde*, tell me what movements are employed in the *Pavane*.

Arbeau. The *Pavane* is easy to dance, because it is only two *simples* and a *double* advancing, and two *simples* and a *double* retiring; and it is played in duple time. And observe that in dancing it the two *simples* and the *double* advancing are begun with the left foot; and the two *simples* and the *double* retiring are begun with the right.

Capriol. Then the tabor and other instruments play eight bars for the advance and eight for the retreat?

Arbeau. That is so, and if you wish you need not retire at all, but keep going forward all the time.

Capriol. Are there no retreats in the *Basse-Danse?*

Arbeau. Sometimes the throng is so great and there are so many people in the room that the space for dancing is limited so that when you are near the end of the room you must do one of two things, either you and the damsel you lead must retreat or you must make a *conversion.*[1]

Capriol. What do you mean by a *conversion?*

Arbeau. It means that on nearing the end of the room, you make the damsel keep on advancing and you retreat as far as she advances until your back is turned to the side you formerly faced.

Capriol. Which of the two courses seems to you the better?

Arbeau. In my opinion, it is better to make a *conversion* so that the damsel can see where she is going, for if she should meet with some hindrance in making the retreat, she might fall, an occurrence which would bring censure upon you and lower you in her good graces. Hence, it seems to me, *Pavanes* ought to be done, when one wishes to dance them, by making two or three circles round the room.

Capriol. Is the drum-rhythm for the *Pavane* the same as that of the *Basse-Danse?*

Arbeau. It is in duple time, consisting of a crotchet and two quavers in this manner:

Capriol. I find these *Pavanes* and *Basses-Danses* fine, stately and well suited to honourable persons, especially to ladies and young girls.

Arbeau. A nobleman can dance the *Pavane* with cape and

[1] Literally *a wheel round.*

sword, and you others dressed in your long gowns, walking decorously with a studied gravity, and the damsel with chaste demeanour and eyes cast down, sometimes glancing at the onlookers with a virginal modesty. And as for the *Pavane*, it is used by kings, princes and great lords, to display themselves on some day of solemn festival with their fine mantles and robes of ceremony; and then the queens and the princesses and the great ladies accompany them with the long trains of their dresses let down and trailing behind them, or sometimes carried by damsels. And these *Pavanes*, played by hautboys and sackbuts, are called the *Grand Bal*, and last until those who dance have circled two or three times round the room, if they do not prefer to dance by advances and retreats. These *Pavanes* are also used in a masquerade when there is a procession of triumphal chariots of gods and goddesses, emperors or kings resplendent with majesty.

Capriol. Put in writing for me the airs of a *Pavane* and a *Basse-Danse.*

Arbeau. I am quite willing to do so in my desire that such honourable dances should displace the lascivious and shameless ones which have been introduced in their stead to the sorrow of wise lords, ladies and dames of good and modest judgment. First, I will give you a *Pavane* with the drum-rhythm in slow, duple time, accompanied with the alto, tenor and bass, which will enable you to know how to dance all the others ; and, if you wish, you can have it sung or played in four-part harmony without dancing it. Then I shall give you a common *Basse-Danse* with its *retour* and *tordion*, which likewise will serve you as a pattern for all the others. Then you will know by heart what I have given you in writing above.

Pavane in four parts, with the drum-rhythm.

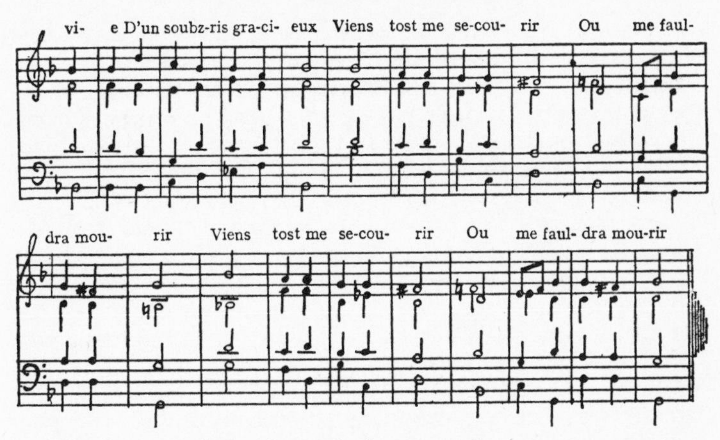

The *Pavane* given above, in four-part harmony, comprises two advances and two retreats marked by their characters thus : **ss d ss d ss d ss d**, and takes thirty-two bars and drum-rhythms. And, to lengthen it, you must repeat it as many times as it pleases the musicians or the dancers and, as one day you may wish to sing the whole song, here are the words.

Belle qui tiens ma vie
Captive dans tes yeulx
Qui m'as l'ame ravie
D'un soubz-ris gracieux
Viens tost me secourir
Ou me fauldra mourir.

Pourquoi fuis tu, mignarde
Si je suis près de toy
Quand tes yeulx je regarde
Je me perds dedans moy
Car tes perfections
Changent mes actions.

Tes beautez & ta grace
Et tes divins propos
Ont eschauffé la glace
Qui me geloit les os
Et ont remply mon cœur
D'une amoureuse ardeur.

Mon ame souloit estre
Libre de passions
Mais amour s'est faict maistre
De mes affections,
Et a mis soubs sa loy
Et mon cœur & ma foy.

Approche donc ma belle,
Approche toy mon bien,
Ne me sois plus rebelle
Puisque mon cœur est tien,
Pour mon mal appaiser
Donne moy un baiser.

Je meurs mon Angelette
Je meurs en te baisant
Ta bouche tant doucette
Va mon bien ravissant.
A ce coup mes espritz
Sont tous d'amour espris.

Plustost on verra l'onde
Contre mont reculer,
Et plustost l'œil du monde
Cessera de brusler,
Que l'amour qui m'epoinct
Decroisse d'un seul poinct.

Capriol. This *Pavane* dance is too grave and solemn to dance alone in a room with a young girl.

Arbeau. The musicians sometimes play it less gravely and in a quicker measure, and in this manner it partakes of the moderate *tempo* of a *Basse-Danse*, when it is called *Passamezzo*.[1] A little while ago a new one was introduced called the *Pavane d'Espagne* or Spanish *Pavane*, which is a dance interspersed with a variety of steps and gestures. And because it has some resemblance to the dance called *Canaries*, I shall not explain this dance to you until we come to the latter, only you will understand for the present that there are dancers who quicken the *double* which follows the two *simples*. For where the *double* would consist of only four bars of four minims, they divide[2] it into eight crotchets or sixteen quavers, and consequently make many positions of the feet, passages,[3] and *fleurets*, which have the same cadence and take the same length of time; and such lightly executed divisions and movements of the feet detract from the gravity of the *Pavane*, especially as it is usual for the *Pavane* to be succeeded by the *Galliarde*, which is a light dance.

Capriol. Teach me all these passages and divisions.

Arbeau. All you wish to know is how to divide a *double* according to the tabulation. Good dancers who are agile and lively can make such divisions as seem good to them, so long as they come down on the cadence, as I have told you, in time, with the foot ready to dance the two *simples* which follow the *double*. And sometimes they anticipate their passages on the second *simple*. You will understand these passages and divisions when you know the fashions and diverse manners of moving the feet, which we will speak of when explaining the dance called *Gaillarde*. However, I will give you here in writing the air of a common *Basse-Danse* with the drum-rhythm in triple time.

Capriol. Is it necessary that the tabor and flute be used for *Pavanes* and *Basses-Danses?*

Arbeau. Not unless you so desire. For the airs can be

[1] A description of the Passa-mezzo will be found in Fabritio Caroso da Sermoneta's *Il Ballarino*, 1581.

[2] To "divide" a step was to substitute quicker and more elaborate footing for the ordinary simple steps of the *double*.

[3] A "passage" was a combination of steps or *enchaînement*, to employ the terminology of the academic ballet.

played on viols, spinets, transverse flutes and flutes with nine holes, hautboys and all manner of instruments. It is possible also to sing them. But the tabor is a wonderful help, on account of its regular rhythm, which enables the feet to come into position according as the movements require.

Basse-Danse called *Jouyssance vous donneray*: with the drum-rhythm.

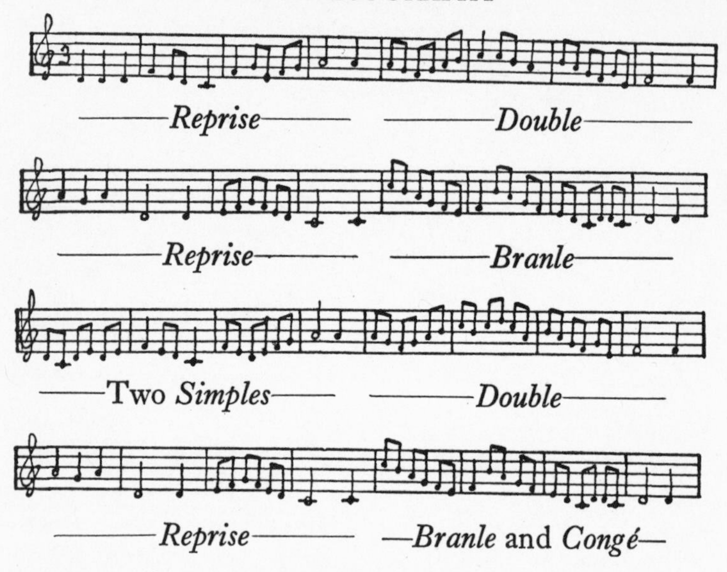

As soon as you hear the last beat of the *branle* which precedes the *congé* you will turn your body towards the damsel, doffing your bonnet and making a *révérence*, to take your *congé* and lead her to the place where the *basse-danse* began, so as to dance the *retour de la basse-danse* according to the drum-rhythms and movements which follow :

Retour de la basse-danse : with the drum-rhythm.

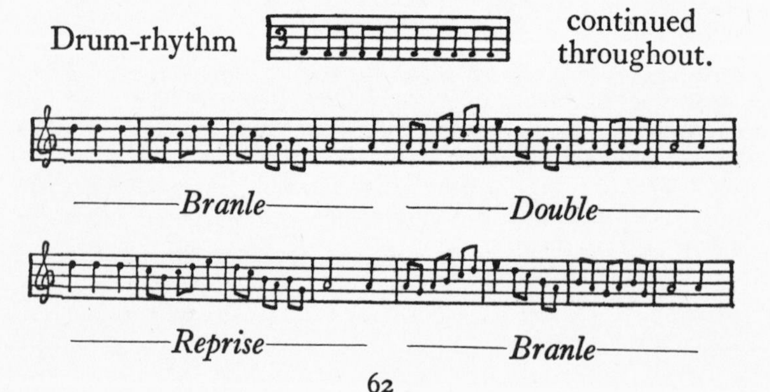

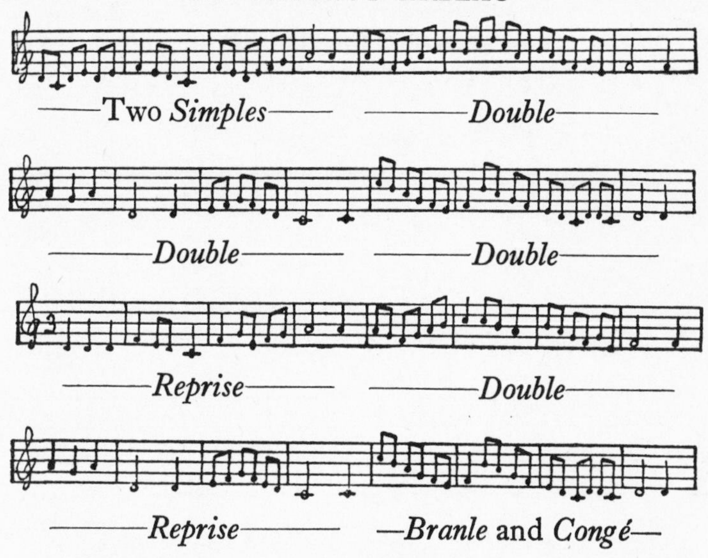

Capriol. I should have liked you to put in writing for me five or six *Pavanes* and as many *Basses-Danses.*

Arbeau. You will find a sufficiently large number of them in the books of dances printed by the late M. Attaignant, who resided near the Church of Saint Cosmo at Paris, and in the books of the late Master Nicolas du Chemin, printer at Paris at the sign of the Silver Lion. All the same you will have to rearrange in triple time all the *Basses-Danses* which are set in duple time.

Capriol. What prevents your rearranging them in this manner and giving them to me in writing ?

Arbeau. When one knows all the steps and movements of a *Pavane* and of a common *Basse-Danse*, one can dance all the others. Because however different their airs may be, whether sung or played, they are all of the same number of bars. It is the duty of the instrumentalists, then, to learn the various kinds, and, as for yourself, it should be sufficient for you to know how to dance them. This is easy for you now, as you have learned and understood them.

Capriol. You are forgetting to tell me of the uncommon and irregular *Basses-Danses*.

Arbeau. They have no other kinds of movements than the common and differ only in that they are longer or shorter, or even equal, but the movements are arranged differently to those in a common *Basse-Danse*. Arena has made a list of them which I shall not detail here, because they are rarely danced, and for the moment it is sufficient that you should know the ordinary kind. All the same, I will give you three in writing. One of twenty-four quaternions, which is the longest, one of fourteen quaternions, which is the shortest, and one of twenty quaternions like the ordinary *Basses-Danses*.

Tabulation of the movements for the *Basse-Danse* called *Confortez-moy*, of twenty-four quaternions containing ninety-six bars.

R b ss d ss r b ss d ss r b ss ddd ss r b ss d ss r b c

Tabulation of the movements for the *Basse-Danse* called *Toute-frelore*, of fourteen quaternions containing fifty-six bars and drum-rhythms.

R b ss d ss r b ss ddd ss r b c

Tabulation of the movements for the *Basse-Danse* called *Patience*, of twenty quaternions (like the common *Basse-Danse*) containing eighty bars and drum-rhythms, but which nevertheless is irregular.

R b ss d r d ss r b ss ddd r b ss d ss r b c

I wanted to describe these three to you to serve as examples for all the others, to which, however, you need attach no great importance because few persons danced them in the past and those only who wished to set themselves above others and demonstrate their good memory. And, by such means, they often deceived those who knew how to dance the common ones only, for, as soon as they saw that another wished to dance with them, they asked for one of the irregular ones.

Capriol. Can several persons dance together ?

Arbeau. You could, if it should please you, take two damsels. But one is sufficient and the familiar proverb says that : " He who has two in hand has one too many." Similarly, when you are placed at one end of the room with a damsel, another can take up his position with his mistress at the other end to dance opposite to you. And when one couple approaches the other, they must retreat or make use of the *conversion*. I have explained already what is meant by the latter term.

Capriol. You told me that after the *basse-danse* and its *retour*, the *tordion* must be danced, and that the *tordion* was a kind of *Gaillarde* and you put off speaking to me of the former until you came to the latter.

Arbeau. Those who dance the *Gaillarde* to-day in the towns dance it confusedly and are content with making the five steps and some passages without any order, and care for nothing so long as they make the cadence in time, so much so that the greater part of their best passages is unnoticed and lost. Formerly they were danced with the greatest care. For after the dancer had chosen a damsel, and they had taken their position at the end of the room, they made after the *révérence* one or two circles round the room, simply walking. Then the dancer released the damsel, whereupon she went dancing to the end of the room, where she remained dancing in the same place. Thereafter the dancer who followed her came and stood before her and made some passages turning, if he wished, sometimes to the right, sometimes to the left. This done, she danced up to the other end of the room, where her partner, dancing all the time, went to seek her to make some other passages in front of her. And, continuing these goings and comings, the dancer made new passages to exhibit his skill until the musicians stopped playing. Then, taking the damsel by the hand, he performed the *révérence* and, thanking her, led her to the place whence he had taken her.

Capriol. This manner of dancing seems to me more praiseworthy than the careless performances one generally sees, because each time the dancer turns his back to the damsel, or almost does so, she turns her back to him while he makes some passages.

Arbeau. For some time the *Gaillarde* has been danced

in a manner which they call the *Lyonaise*, in which the dancer, ceding his place to another, takes his *congé* of the damsel and retires. She, thus left alone, continues to dance a little longer, then goes to choose another partner and after having danced with him also, she takes her *congé* and retires. And these changes continue as long as the *Gaillarde* lasts.

Capriol. If there be not enough damsels or dancers for these changes may one choose from those who have danced already ?

Arbeau. You could do so. But this manner has been introduced so that all the damsels in the company may take part in the dance, to discourage the evil custom of those who, indiscreet in their affections, always wish to take the one who is their favourite ; but, by means of these changes, the least favoured can take part in the dance.

Capriol. What movements are necessary to this dance called the *Gaillarde ?*

Arbeau. The *Gaillarde* is so called because one must be blithe and lively to dance it. And when it is danced by a suitable person the movements are lively, though it must be slower for a tall man than for a short one, for the reason that the tall one takes a longer time to execute his steps and to move his legs forward and backward than the short one. It includes the *tordion* which, as we have said above, must be danced after the *retour de la basse-danse*, but the *tordion* is danced more quietly and with less violent actions and gestures.

Capriol. What movements are used in the *Gaillarde* and *tordion ?*

Arbeau. The *Gaillarde* ought to consist of six steps, seeing that it contains six crotchets played in two bars of triple time, thus :—

All the same, there are only five steps, because the fifth and penultimate note is lost in the air, as you see below, where it is replaced by a rest of the same value. Thus there remain only five notes. And in reckoning a step to each note, five must be counted and no more.

Capriol. Then that is what I hear said so often that the dancer of the *Gaillarde* must before all things know his five steps. But how are these five steps executed ?

Arbeau. There are many kinds of steps, by the different combinations of which a diversity of passages are devised. And to each of these is assigned an appropriate name.

Capriol. You have named and taught them to me above. Are they not *révérence*, *branle*, two *simples*, *double* and *reprise*, which you have denoted in writing by the characters **R b ss d r.**

Arbeau. The steps in the *Gaillarde* and the *tordion* are different, as I shall explain to you, and not unreasonably, because the steps and movements of the *Pavane* and *Basse-Danse* are slow and solemn. And those of the *Gaillarde* and *tordion* are light and gay, so that young men of your age are more adapted for dancing them than old greybeards like myself, and to make the explanation clearer I will give you pictures of them, with their names written above, if you find it good and expedient to have them.

Capriol. I pray you devise them so that I may easily understand whatsoever you please to teach me ; and do not be sparing in the matter of pictures, since I find them a great help to the understanding of your words and an aid to memory.

Arbeau. At the commencement of the *Gaillarde* you must presuppose that the dancer, holding the damsel by the hand, makes the *révérence* at the moment when the musicians begin to play ; the *révérence* done, he assumes a goodly modest attitude. To perform the *révérence* you will keep the left foot firmly on the ground and, bending the right knee, carry the point of the toe a little to the rear of the left foot, at the same time doffing your bonnet or hat and saluting your damsel and the company as you see in this picture.

Révérence

When the *révérence* has been performed, straighten the body and replace your bonnet; then, drawing back your right foot, bring and keep the two feet together (*pieds joints*[1]). This is considered to be a correct position when the two feet are so disposed that one is on the right of the other, as you see in the picture below, the toes in a straight line, so that the body is equally balanced on the two feet.

And if it should happen that one foot be so placed as to support the whole weight of the body and the heel of the other foot be brought close up to it so that the toe points at an oblique angle, this pose will be called *pieds joints oblique*, of which there are two kinds. That is to say, *pieds joints, oblique droit*,[2] when the left foot supports the weight of the body and the right rests at an oblique angle to it, and *pieds*

[1] Literally *feet together.*

[2] Literally *feet together, right oblique.*

Pieds joints

joints, oblique gauche,[1] when the right supports the body and the left rests at an oblique angle to it.

Capriol. You do not tell me the degree of this oblique angle and I do not ask without cause, since geometricians hold that between two lines at right angles there are an infinity of oblique lines.

Arbeau. The degree of the oblique angle is left to the will of the dancer; he will place the free foot against the foot which supports the body, either at right angles to it or at any intermediate angle, as it pleases him. For we cannot naturally turn the foot beyond a right angle. Here are the pictures of the movements *pieds joints oblique.*

Pieds joints, oblique droit

Pieds joints, oblique gauche

[1] Literally *feet together, left oblique.*

These movements *pieds joints* will teach you that there are contrary movements which we call *pieds largis*,[1] which occur when the two feet are placed on the ground so that the weight of the body is equally divided, but, instead of being together, they are separated; but not in a forced and cramped manner like the feet of the colossus representing the statue of the Sun cast in copper by Colossus or Chares [2]—pupils of Lysippus—erected at Rhodes, being seventy cubits high, which is equal to about one hundred and five of our Langres feet. This colossus had the legs separated as far as they could naturally be, so that ships could easily pass between them.

Capriol. Then it is not without reason that it was numbered among the wonders of the world, and it was a great misfortune that fifty-six years later it fell owing to an earthquake. I should have liked to have seen the statue to ascertain the truth of what has been written about it, that few people could be found capable of embracing its thumb. But, apart from this story, I quite understand that you wish the movement *pieds largis* to be done so that the feet are neither too wide apart, nor too close to one another, nor joined together.

Pieds largis

Arbeau. This movement and position *pieds largis* is also made when one foot supports the weight of the body and the

[1] Literally *feet apart.*

[2] Chares of Lindus in Rhodes, a sculptor in bronze, was the favourite pupil of Lysippus. Chares flourished at the beginning of the third century B.C. His chief work was the statue of Apollo known as "The Colossus of Rhodes," celebrated as one of the Seven Wonders of the World. It took twelve years to erect, and cost 300 talents. It was overthrown by an earthquake and broken to pieces 56 years later, in 224 B.C.

other rests at an oblique angle to it. This can be done in two ways. Either, the feet being separated, when the left supports the dancer's body and the right rests at an oblique angle to it, which is called *pieds largis, oblique droit*[1]; or, contrariwise, when the right foot supports the body and the left rests at an oblique angle to it; this is called *pieds largis, oblique gauche*.[2]

Pieds largis, oblique droit

Pieds largis, oblique gauche

Capriol. You have shown me six different positions and movements; which do you consider the most suitable?

Arbeau. One of those where the foot rests at an oblique angle seems to me the most beautiful, because we see on medals and antique statues that men standing on one foot look the more artistic and more pleasing. And when the feet are joined or separated in a straight line they have something feminine in their pose. And thus, while it is unbecoming for a damsel to assume a mannish pose, a man must also avoid effeminate attitudes. You can mark this in *révérences*, because, in performing them, one foot is brought smartly to the rear so that it is crossed behind the other and the damsels slightly bend both knees and then straighten them. And while I am concerned with *révérences*, I wish to tell you that the *révérences* of salutation which are made at the beginning, at the end, and sometimes in the middle of the dances, are not included among lively move-

[1] Literally *feet apart, right oblique*. [2] Literally *feet apart, left oblique*.

ments, although two other kinds of passing *révérences* are included, that is to say, used in certain passages of the *Gaillarde*.

Capriol. What is the difference between these passing *révérences* and those of salutation ?

Arbeau. In the passing *révérence*, the bonnet or hat must not be doffed, and although it is done in almost the same manner, by bending the knee and carrying one foot to the rear, it is done in a shorter space of time, as you will learn later. There are two kinds of them, one when, the left foot supporting the body, the right is crossed behind. This is called *révérence passagière droite.*[1] The other is when, the right foot supporting the body, the left is crossed behind, which is called *révérence·passagière gauche.*[2]

Révérence passagière droite

Révérence passagière gauche

Continuing the designation of steps and movements, I shall say that there is a movement called *pied croisé*,[3] when one springs on one foot to support the body and at the same time carries the other in the air in front of the shin. This is done in two ways ; either the left foot supports the body, and the right is crossed in front of the left shin, which is called *pied croisé droit*[4] ; or, contrariwise, when the right foot supports the body and the left is crossed in front of the right shin, which is called *pied croisé gauche.*[5]

[1] Literally *passing bow, right.*
[2] Literally *passing bow, left.*
[3] Literally *foot crossed.*
[4] Literally *foot crossed right.*
[5] Literally *foot crossed left.*

Pied croisé droit *Pied croisé gauche*

Capriol. There are indeed many kinds of gestures and movements.

Arbeau. You are anxious, that I can understand, to begin to perform the Five Steps, but it cannot be helped, you must have the patience to listen to the manner of executing all the movements. Because you know that in the art of grammar the pupil first collects nouns, verbs and other parts of speech, then he learns to use them together with congruity. Hence, in the art of dancing, you must first learn many particular movements, then, by means of the airs and tabulations of the movements, which will be written out for you, all will be clear.

Capriol. Could I not make combinations according to my fancy when I know the particular movements?

Arbeau. You could do so, but you could not perform them unless you had communicated them beforehand to good dancers, and it is much better to make a collection of passages already invented and accepted, for there is a certain grace in some which is not found in others.

Capriol. Continue, if you please, the rest of the movements?

Arbeau. Sometimes, having sprung on one foot, and placed it to support the body, one brings the toe of the other foot against the one on the ground; this movement is called *marque pied*, that is to say, *marque pied droit* [1] when the right foot is moved: and *marque pied gauche* [2] when the left.

[1] Literally *mark right foot* (toe). [2] Literally *mark left foot* (toe).

Marque pied droit

Marque pied gauche

When, on the contrary, having sprung on one foot, and placed it to support the body, one brings the heel of the other foot against the one on the ground, this movement is termed *marque talon droit* [1] when the right heel is moved; and *marque talon gauche* [2] when the left.

Marque talon droit

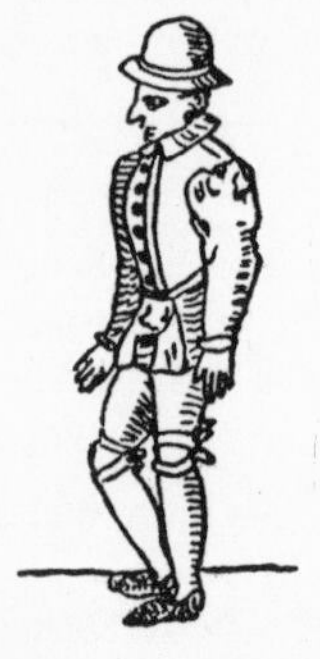

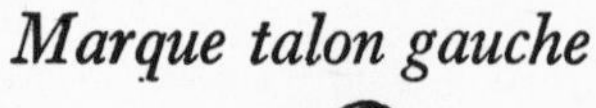

Marque talon gauche

Capriol. Regarding the designation of the movement *marque talon*, it seems to me that it is well named, but then you should call the preceding movement *marque orteil* [3] and not *marque pied*.[4]

Arbeau. You are right, and if you wish you can call it so. But I have used the other because the expression *marque orteil* is harsher and more troublesome to pronounce.

[1] Literally *mark right heel.*
[2] Literally *mark left heel.*
[3] Literally *mark toe.*
[4] Literally *mark foot.*

Capriol. The Poles, as I have heard it said, customarily walk on their toes.

Arbeau. Their heels are supported and raised by the cork or iron placed on their shoes, so that they cannot run as lightly as ourselves. And, if you look about you, you will find that all animals, with few exceptions, progress in this manner. That is the reason why the Poles appear two or three inches taller than they really are.

To return to the question of the movements of the *Gaillarde*, you must know further that there is a certain movement and position of the feet which we call *coup de pied* [1] or *grue*,[2] when the dancer springs on one foot to support the body and raises the other forward in the air as if he wished to kick some one. And such a movement can be made in two ways, that is to say, with the right foot raised, which is called *grue droite*,[3] and with the left foot raised, which is called *grue gauche*.[4]

Sometimes the foot is raised only a small distance from the ground and is not carried forward or only very little. This is called *pied en l'air droit*,[5] if the right foot be raised; or *pied en l'air gauche*,[6] if the left be raised.

One picture will serve for the two movements, only you must remember that when you find in the tabulation the words *pied en l'air*, the movement should be made very close to the ground and gently, as a damsel would do it. These are the steps and movements used in dancing the *tordion*. And when you find in the tabulation the word *grue*, the foot should be raised very high and in a bold manner.

Capriol. I shall very carefully commit this advice to memory and recall also the reason for it which you gave me above, because in dancing the *tordion* the damsel is always held by the hand. And whoever dances the *tordion* clumsily gives trouble and is a burden to the damsel.

Arbeau. At the present time, dancers have none of these modest considerations in their *Voltes* and other similarly

[1] Literally *forward kick*.
[2] Literally *crane*. Possibly the term is derived from the movements of the crane when walking. A *grue* may be rendered more clearly as a raising of either foot to the fourth position front, *en l'air* (*demi-position*).
[3] *Kick forward with right foot.*
[4] *Kick forward with left foot.*
[5] Literally *foot in the air, right*, i.e. *right foot in the air*.
[6] Literally *foot in the air, left*, i.e. *left foot in the air*.

lascivious and wayward dances which have been brought into use, in the dancing of which the damsels are made to jump in such a manner that they very often show their bare knees if they do not keep one hand on their dresses to prevent it.

Capriol. This manner of dancing seems to me neither beautiful nor decent, unless you are dancing with some buxom serving wench.

Arbeau. I shall not fail to give you hereafter the tabulation for dancing it. However, here are the pictures of the movements *grue* and *pied en l'air*.

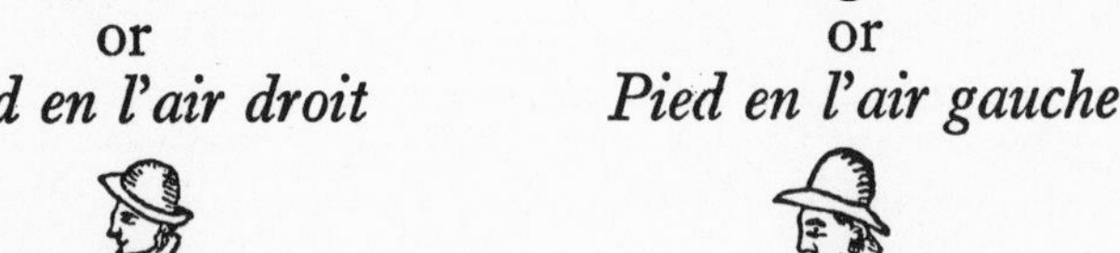

Grue droite or *Pied en l'air droit*

Grue gauche or *Pied en l'air gauche*

The *grue* is sometimes done so that when the dancer springs and places one foot in the place previously occupied by the other foot, the latter is raised forward in the air. This movement is called *entretaille*,[1] and is also of two kinds, as there are two kinds of *grue*. That is to say, *entretaille du gauche*, making a *grue droit*, and *entretaille du droit*, making a *grue gauche*.

Capriol. I quite understand this; it is only the same movement, except that it begins with this *entretaille*.

Arbeau. A movement contrary to the *grue* is made when the dancer springs on one foot to support his body and raises

[1] Mr. Charles d'Albert defines *entretaille* as the jump preceding any step. *Cf.* C. d'Albert, *Encyclopædia of Dancing*, N.D., p. 56.

the other backwards, and this movement is called *ruade*.[1] That is to say, *ruade droite* [2] if the right foot be raised backwards, and *ruade gauche* [3] if the left.

Ruade droite *Ruade gauche*

If one foot be raised by the side of the other and not forward like the *grue*, nor backwards as in the *ruade*, this movement is called *ru de vache*,[4] because cows kick sideways and not backward like horses. There are also two varieties of this step, *ru de vache droit*,[5] when the left foot is sprung upon to support the body, and the right is raised; and *ru de vache gauche*,[6] when the right is sprung upon to support the body and the left raised.

Capriol. The movement *ru de vache* is rarely used, I believe.

Arbeau. That is true, it is seldom practised; but I cannot omit it, since I wish to leave nothing undone while we are concerned with the movements and steps of the *Gaillarde*. And this is not employed in the *Gaillarde* alone, but also in other dances of which we will speak later on.

Capriol. This will have been done when you come to speak of the other dances.

Arbeau. There will be some little differences to be considered.

[1] Literally *kick* (*by a horse*); i.e. *a backward kick*.
[2] Literally *kick backward with right foot*.
[3] Literally *kick backward with left foot*.
[4] Literally *cow kick*; i.e. *sideways kick*.
[5] *Kick sideways with right foot*.
[6] *Kick sideways with left foot*.

Capriol. What differences ?

Arbeau. I will tell you when we come to them. For the present, look at the pictures of the two kinds of *ru de vache* of which I lately spoke to you.

Ru de vache droit

Ru de vache gauche

When both feet are sprung upon and placed on the ground, one forward and one backward, both supporting the dancer's body, this bearing and movement is called position or *posture*, which generally serves to mark a cadence. This can be done in two ways. When the right foot is in front, it is called *posture droite* ; [1] and when the left foot is in front, it is called *posture gauche*.[2] And observe this counsel regarding these *postures*, that they are more graceful when, in the execution of them, the rear foot is placed on the ground just a little sooner than the one in front ; for when both come down together, it is as though a sack of corn were dumped on the ground.

Posture droite

Posture gauche

[1] Literally *right posture*.

[2] Literally *left posture*.

Capriol. I have noticed that in all these movements mentioned above, there is always one or both feet on the ground.

Arbeau. That is so. And certainly those in which only one foot is on the ground are more lively. But there is a movement called *saut*,[1] which is done when both feet are off the ground and raised in the air, which is still more lively. And you must understand that there are two kinds of *saut*, that is to say, *saut majeur* [2] and *petit saut*.[3] When it is a *petit saut* it is part and parcel of the movements, and is not specially noted in the tabulation.

Capriol. I do not understand at all what you say.

Arbeau. Imagine that you are in the position *pieds joints*. If the tabulation bids you make a *grue droite*, what would you do ?

Capriol. I should support my body on the left foot and raise the right foot forward in the air.

Arbeau. The *grue droite* may be done so, but it will not be lively. That is why instead of leaving the left foot on the ground, you must place it there a second time. And to do this, it is necessary to make a *petit saut* on the left foot. In doing so, you will see clearly enough that the *saut* is, as I told you, part of the movement called *grue*. And thus the *petit saut* must be used in all the other steps and movements where one foot is raised in the air, and also, if you remember, I have told you that you must spring on both feet and place them in position. For this reason, when I give you in writing the tabulation of the *Gaillarde*, I shall not mention the *petit saut*, and you will only write down the steps and movements, for it is understood that the *petit saut* is included in them.

Capriol. What is a *saut majeur ?*

Arbeau. It is a separate movement which precedes the cadence, and will be noted and numbered in the tabulation of the *Gaillarde* by a rest, which takes the place of one of the six crotchets of triple time of which the *Gaillarde* consists ; so that the *saut majeur* is of equal duration to one of the other five steps or movements.

[1] Literally *jump*. [2] Literally *big jump*. Literally *little jump*.

Capriol. To perform a complete Five Steps, you must execute four movements, then a *saut majeur*, then the *posture ?*

Arbeau. That is true when the cadence is made, which musicians call *clausula ;* and there are many dancers so agile that, in making the *saut majeur*, they move their legs in the air, and this shaking is called *capriole*,[1] as you see in this picture below. But it must be done so dexterously that it does not delay the *posture* which, in the ordinary way, follows the *saut majeur* in making this cadence.

Capriole

Capriol. I shall be glad to learn this *capriole*, since it bears my name. But what do you mean by cadence ?

Arbeau. Cadence is simply a *saut majeur* followed by a *posture*. And just as in the performance of music, the instrumentalists having played the penultimate chord, delay a little the concluding one to make a pleasant and harmonious close ; even so the *saut majeur*, which is almost like a silence of the feet and pause in the movements, is the reason why the *posture* which follows it has a better grace and is found the more agreeable. Further, you can understand that if the dancer does not perform this *saut*, he must execute movements which would be six in number, one for each of the six crotchets of the *Gaillarde*, and thus would fall always in cadence on the same side. But this does not happen on account of the *saut*, which makes the number of the move-

[1] Literally *caper*. *Capriole* or *cabriole* is derived from the Italian *capriola,* caper. *Cf. capriolo,* wild goat, and the Latin *capriolus*.

ments and steps uneven, and consequently the cadence falls first on one side then on the other.

Capriol. What is the objection to making all the cadences on the same side ?

Arbeau. Do you not know that there is pleasure in variety and that the same thing repeated is odious, according to the well-known phrase about warmed-up cabbage.[1] And the verse of Horace so often quoted :

Ridetur chorda qui semper oberrat eadem.[2]

Capriol. Is this cadence always made on the sixth crotchet ?

Arbeau. As a general rule it is most frequently made thus, though there are certainly some qualifications to make. But I will speak to you of these when we come to them. For the present I will say this, that the dancer executes six positions and movements of the feet, one to each of the six notes, and passes over the cadence, reserving it until the twelfth beat, keeping the rest on the eleventh for the *saut*, and thus the passage remains one of eleven steps. And if the dancer wishes, he can pass over the cadence until the eighteenth beat, making the *saut majeur* on the rest which falls on the seventeenth, which then becomes a passage of seventeen steps. The dancer can again pass over the cadence and reserve it until the twenty-fourth, or the thirtieth, or thirty-sixth beat, and so he makes passages of twenty-three, twenty-nine and thirty-five steps. But I counsel you not to employ them, because the onlookers would be tired of waiting so long for the cadence, and would think that you were out of your mind. And, in truth, the memory would be troubled by such long passages.

Capriol. Are these all the steps and movements which are employed in the *Gaillarde ?*

Arbeau. These are the ones I call to mind at present. If, while observing some good performers, you notice that they execute others, you will set them down in writing and accord them such names as seem good to you.

[1] *Crambe repetita* (literally *warmed-up cabbage,* meaning stale repetition).
[2] Who'd play and sing,
Is laughed at, that still jarreth on one string.

Capriol. Well, here I am, holding a damsel by the hand; my *révérence* is made, my bonnet replaced, and my features composed. In what manner shall I begin?

Arbeau. You will make your steps and movements according to the tabulation which you have committed to memory. But I would counsel you to be modest: that is to say, to dance close to the ground, to make the five steps quietly, as if you were dancing the *tordion*, and, further, to make a circle round the room, holding your damsel the while. Then, taking your *congé* when you are so inclined, you will let her dance alone, and begin to dance your five steps higher from the ground until you return in front of her. Then, in lively spirits, you will make such passages as please you. For, if you spring too gaily at the beginning, it would seem as if you wished to break, as the proverb says, a chitterling across your knee.

Capriol. I have seen many people who assume affected attitudes before beginning to dance.

Arbeau. I do not like this fashion, because such people expose themselves to the rebuke of the poet:

Quid dignum tanto feret hic promissor hiatu.[1]

Capriol. First, give me the air of a *tordion*, then of a *Gaillarde*.

Arbeau. The air of a *tordion* and that of a *Gaillarde* are the same, and there is no difference between them except that the *tordion* is danced close to the ground in a lighter and more animated *tempo*, while the *Gaillarde* is danced with high steps to a slower and weightier measure. All the same, you are quite right to ask for the air of a *tordion*, for when the dancer knows the airs and sings them in his mind with the musician, he cannot fail to dance them well. You will take then the air which follows as a pattern for all other *tordions*, of which there is a very great variety.

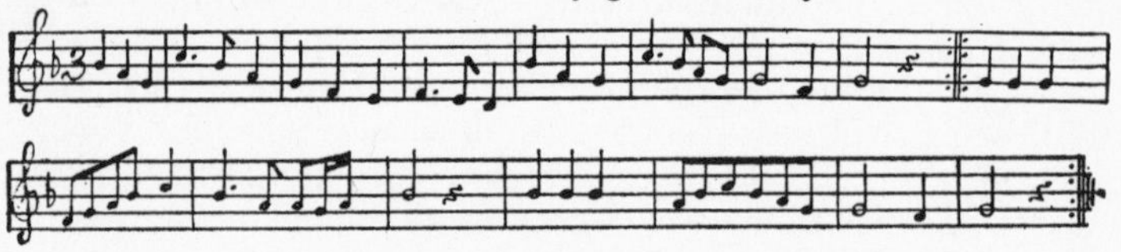

Capriol. I know this air well, but I do not perceive the cadences of which you spoke to me.

[1] What doth this promiser such gaping worth afford?

Arbeau. I have marked the positions of the cadences by perpendicular bars, and you can yourself reduce the air to the following form.

Capriol. I understand it much better than I did; now I have only to know what movements to set to it.

Arbeau. Execute *pied en l'air gauche* to the first crotchet, for the first step. Then *pied en l'air droit* to the second crotchet, for the second step. Then *pied en l'air gauche* to the third crotchet, for the third step. Then *pied en l'air droit* to the fourth crotchet, for the fourth step. On the rest that takes the place of a crotchet, make a moderate *saut*, supposing that it is a *tordion* which you dance; execute a *posture gauche* to the last crotchet for the fifth step.

Continuing your *tordion*, change and execute to the right everything that you did to the left and *vice versâ*, that is to say:—

Execute *pied en l'air droit* to the first crotchet, for the first step. Then *pied en l'air gauche* to the second crotchet, for the second step. Then *pied en l'air droit* to the third crotchet, for the third step. Then *pied en l'air gauche* to the fourth crotchet, for the fourth step. On the rest that takes the place of a crotchet, make the *saut majeur* which precedes the *posture*. But you will make the *saut* a moderate one if you are dancing the *tordion* and not the *Gaillarde*.

Execute a *posture droite* to the last crotchet, for the fifth step. And so long as the musician continues to play, continue making your cadences on alternate sides, coming to the ground alternately in *posture gauche* and *posture droite*. And in order that everything may be easy for you to understand, I will give you here a tabulation of what I have just said, which will show you the whole at a glance; for I will write you out the air of this *tordion* again, and against each note I will set down the necessary steps and movements. And it is my intention to do the same for the air of a *Gaillarde*. This tabulation will serve you for all the other *Gaillardes*, which are also innumerable.

Capriol. When the player has finished the *tordion*, is it not necessary to make a *révérence* of salutation when taking *congé* of the damsel ?

Arbeau. Yes, you should courteously lead her back to the place from which you took her, thanking her the while for the honour she has done you.

Tabulation of the *Tordion* that follows immediately after the *Retour de la basse-danse*

Air of the *Tordion*

Movements to be made by the dancer in executing the *Tordion*

1. *Pied en l'air gauche.*
2. *Pied en l'air droit.*
3. *Pied en l'air gauche.*
4. *Pied en l'air droit.*
5. *Saut moyen.*
6. *Posture gauche.*

The reverse of the preceding.

1. *Pied en l'air droit.*
2. *Pied en l'air gauche.*
3. *Pied en l'air droit.*
4. *Pied en l'air gauche.*
5. *Saut moyen.*
6. *Posture droite.*

As at the beginning.

1. *Pied en l'air gauche.*
2. *Pied en l'air droit.*
3. *Pied en l'air gauche.*
4. *Pied en l'air droit.*
5. *Saut moyen.*
6. *Posture gauche.*

Reverse.

1. *Pied en l'air droit.*
2. *Pied en l'air gauche.*

3. *Pied in l'air droit.*
4. *Pied en l'air gauche.*
5. *Saut moyen.*
6. *Posture droite.*

The movements *marque pied* and *marque talon* are made very quietly and you could use them in place of the *pieds en l'air* thus :

Air of the *Tordion*

Movements of the five steps of the *Tordion*

A
1. *Marque pied gauche.*
2. *Marque talon gauche.*
3. *Marque pied droit.*
4. *Marque talon droit.*
5. *Saut moyen.*
6. *Posture gauche.*

B
1. *Marque pied droit.*
2. *Marque talon droit.*
3. *Marque pied gauche.*
4. *Marque talon gauche.*
5. *Saut moyen.*
6. *Posture droite.*

Capriol. I am troubled about the position of the cadences. Would it not be sufficient to divide the *tordion* by perpendicular lines so that each section comprised two bars of triple time, and to make a step, *saut majeur* and *posture*, to the last bar ?

Arbeau. It all amounts to the same thing. And I only suggested the reduction to explain your Five Steps more clearly to you. I shall make no further use of this process of reduction, but leave the air of the *Gaillarde* in my tabulation in its original form without omitting anything. Only, remember to employ the steps according to the divisions of time shown with the air. And observe that the cadence will occur as shown in the examples below, of which the third is reduced.

Capriol. Cannot the second bar of triple time which you call cadence consist of music other than one of the three examples which you have noted here ?

Arbeau. It can be of many other kinds, as it pleases the composer and as the air of a *Gaillarde* requires. And it must necessarily be that cadence is made in the second bar or else delayed until the fourth bar (which we have called a passage of eleven steps), or until the sixth bar (which we have called a passage of seventeen steps).

Capriol. It is time you gave me the tabulation of the steps of the *Gaillarde.*

Arbeau. There are so many *Gaillardes* in existence that I do not know which to choose to begin with and use as a foundation. When I first learned to dance at Poitiers, our master played one which he called *La Traditore my fa morire*, which air is held to be the most beautiful of all *Gaillardes.* I will here set down the music of it for you.

Air of the *Gaillarde* called *La Traditore my fa morire*

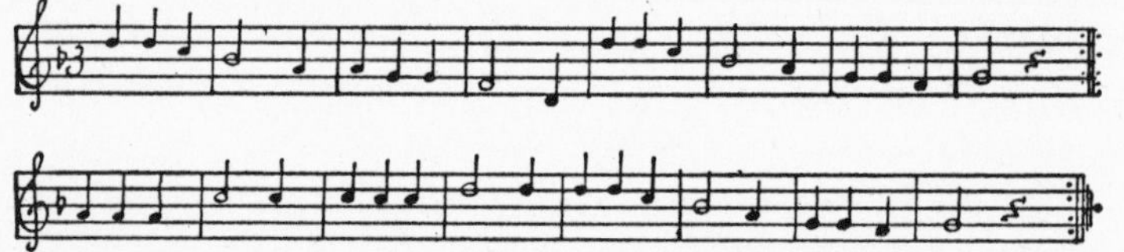

Capriol. I consider this air wonderfully pleasing. When we gave our *Aubades* at Orleans we always played on our lutes and citherns the *Gaillarde* called *La Romanesca.* But to me it has come to seem stale and trivial. I learned one on the lute which I was glad to see danced by my companions, because I knew how to play and sing it, and also it seemed to me that the steps were well marked by those who danced it. It is called *Antoinette.* Here is the music :—

Air of the *Gaillarde* called *Antoinette*

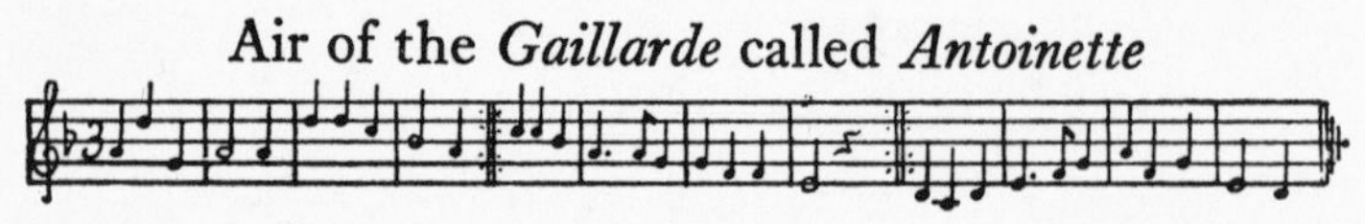

Arbeau. The air of this *Gaillarde Antoinette* is gay indeed. And, as you have it to hand, we will take it to make the first step and found upon it the tabulation of the steps and movements of the *Gaillarde*.

Capriol. Since all the airs of the *Gaillarde* are related, it is all one to me whether you begin with the *Gaillarde Antoinette* or with any other that may please you.

Arbeau. I shall begin my tabulation with your *Gaillarde*. Then I will give you others at random just as they come into my memory.

Tabulation of the Five Steps of the *Gaillarde*, the movements of which are made as in the *tordion*, except that in the execution of them they are done higher and more vigorously, and in the place of the *pied en l'air*, the dancer makes *coups de pied* or *grues*.

Air of the *Gaillarde* called *Antoinette*

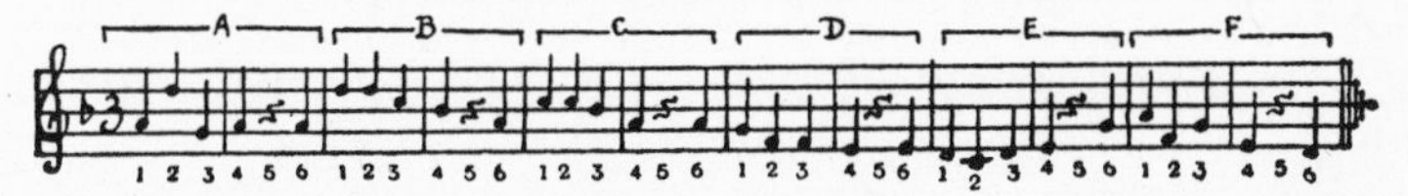

Movements to be made by the dancer in dancing this *Gaillarde*

A
1. *Grue gauche.*
2. *Grue droite.*
3. *Grue gauche.*
4. *Grue droite.*
5. *Saut majeur.*
6. *Posture gauche.*

Reverse.

B
1. *Grue droite.*
2. *Grue gauche.*
3. *Grue droite.*
4. *Grue gauche.*
5. *Saut majeur.*
6. *Posture droite.*

And continue thus by repeating from the beginning.

Another Five Steps

C
1. *Pied croisé droit.*
2. *Pied croisé droit.*
3. *Pied croisé gauche.*
4. *Pied croisé gauche.*
5. *Saut majeur.*
6. *Posture droite.*

Reverse.

D
1. *Pied croisé gauche.*
2. *Pied croisé gauche.*
3. *Pied croisé droit.*
4. *Pied croisé droit.*
5. *Saut majeur.*
6. *Posture gauche.*

And continue thus by repeating from the beginning.

Another Five Steps

E
1. *Grue droite.*
2. *Posture droite* without a *petit saut.*
3. *Entretaille gauche* making a *grue droite.*
4. *Grue gauche.*
5. *Saut majeur.*
6. *Posture droite.*

Reverse.

F
1. *Grue gauche.*
2. *Posture gauche* without a *petit saut.*
3. *Entretaille droite* making a *grue gauche.*
4. *Grue droite.*
5. *Saut majeur.*
6. *Posture gauche.*

And continue thus by repeating from the beginning.

Capriol. Why have you placed a *posture droite* without a *petit saut* on the second crotchet for the second step ?

Arbeau. One must suppose that dancers have found that the addition of some pleasing variation makes the dance more graceful, and, better still, instead of placing both feet on the ground for the said *posture*, they will support themselves on the heel of the foot in front and hold the knee stiff and not bent, for that it is more graceful.

Air of the *Gaillarde* called *Baisons nous belle &c.*

Movements to be made by the dancer in dancing this *Gaillarde*

A

1. *Ruade droite.*
2. *Pied croisé* or *grue gauche.*
3. *Ruade droite.*
4. *Entretaille droite* making a *grue gauche.*
5. *Saut majeur.*
6. *Posture droite.*

Reverse.

B

1. *Ruade gauche.*
2. *Pied croisé* or *grue droite.*
3. *Ruade gauche.*
4. *Entretaille gauche* making a *grue droite.*
5. *Saut majeur.*
6. *Posture gauche.*

And continue thus by repeating from the beginning.

Another Five Steps

C

1. *Pieds joints.*
2. *Grue droite.*
3. *Ruade droite.*
4. *Entretaille droite* making a *grue gauche.*
5. *Saut majeur.*
6. *Posture droite.*

Reverse.

D

1. *Pieds joints.*
2. *Grue gauche.*
3. *Ruade gauche.*
4. *Entretaille gauche* making a *grue droite.*
5. *Saut majeur.*
6. *Posture gauche.*

And continue thus by repeating from the beginning.

In the Five Steps already described, you could replace the *pieds joints* by *postures*, and further, make the *postures* not forward but sideways, as if you executed a *pieds largis*.

Capriol. You say : " continue by repeating the beginning," but, by doing so, one would execute only one kind of Five Steps in a *Gaillarde*.

Arbeau. This may be left to the dancer's pleasure, for, if he wishes, instead of repeating the beginning, he will go forward with a different kind of Five Steps, and he cannot do wrong, provided that he has done the reverse of his first five. And if the dancer finds himself pressed for space, so that there is not sufficient room for him to walk straight forward, he can dance the said Five Steps in a circle, and by turning his body, endeavour to finish in front of his damsel.

Capriol. Should I always dance my Five Steps in a straight line when there is room to do so ?

Arbeau. When I speak of going straight forward, I mean not to turn the body entirely, because you will dance with a good grace if you present first your right, then your left side to the damsel, as if you wished to fence. The *grue droite* should show the right side and the *grue gauche* the left side.

Capriol. I am of the opinion that by combining the different movements which you have shown me, I could devise many varieties of Five Steps out of my own head.

Arbeau. You could certainly do so. But you must observe that some Five Steps are simply called Five Steps because they occupy the same measure of time as the usual Five Steps, and yet they may contain more or less than five movements. And this is due to extended or curtailed note-values. For there are two bars of triple time to each cadence, and each of these two bars contains six crotchet beats, of which one is converted into a rest, making four with the *posture ;* and it follows naturally, if each of the first four notes is divided into two (making eight quavers in place of four crotchets), that, adapting a movement to each note, there will be, prior to the *posture*, eight steps in place of four, which, including the *posture*, will make nine steps in all.

Air of the *Gaillarde* called *Si j'ayme ou non &c.*

A Five Steps of two movements which can be made by the dancer in executing this *Gaillarde*

A
1. *Pieds joints* or *grue droite.*
2. *Saut majeur* with *capriole.*
3. *Posture gauche.*

Reverse.

B
1. *Pieds joints* or *grue gauche.*
2. *Saut majeur* with *capriole.*
3. *Posture droite.*

And continue thus by repeating from the beginning.

You will see from the example above that the *pieds joints* or *grue droite* occupies three crotchet beats, and the *saut majeur*, with the *posture*, takes the remainder of the time; and to arrive at this result the rest on which the *saut majeur* is made is advanced to the fourth beat (instead of the fifth).

Another Five Steps of three movements

C
1. *Grue droite.*
2. *Entretaille droite* making a *grue gauche.*
3. *Saut majeur.*
4. *Posture droite.*

Reverse.

D
1. *Grue gauche.*
2. *Entretaille gauche* making a *grue droite.*
3. *Saut majeur.*
4. *Posture gauche.*

And continue thus by repeating from the beginning.

Mark from the above, that the *grue* takes two crotchet

beats, the *entretaille* making a *grue*, takes two more crotchet beats, the *saut majeur* takes the crotchet rest, and the *posture* takes the time of another crotchet. And thus all these Five Steps are reduced and shortened to three steps, which take the same time as a Five Steps.

Another curtailed Five Steps

E
1. *Révérence gauche.*
2. *Pied croisé gauche.*
3. *Saut majeur.*
4. *Posture droite.*

Reverse.

F
1. *Révérence droite.*
2. *Pied croisé droit.*
3. *Saut majeur.*
4. *Posture gauche.*

And continue thus by repeating from the beginning.

Another curtailed Five Steps

G
1. *Pied croisé droit.*
2. *Entretaille droite* making a *grue gauche.*
3. *Saut majeur.*
4. *Posture droite.*

Reverse.

H
1. *Pied croisé gauche.*
2. *Entretaille gauche* making a *grue droite.*
3. *Saut majeur.*
4. *Posture gauche.*

And continue thus by repeating from the beginning.

Capriol. You must give me an example of a cadence containing more than five steps or movements.

Arbeau. There is an infinite number which you will

practise and learn from those of your own age. For the present, take the seven steps which follow, which are equivalent and reduced to the two bars of triple time required by all Five Steps ; for, as you see in the tabulation, the first and third crotchets, which should not demand more than one step apiece, each have two steps assigned to them, marked in the tabulation by two quavers. And you will notice that two quavers and a crotchet, to which the dancer makes his two *pieds en l'air* and a *grue*, without a *petit saut*, are called a *fleuret*, so that two *fleurets*, a *saut majeur* and a *posture* comprise the Five Steps.

Air of a *Gaillarde*

Movements which can be made by the dancer in executing this *Gaillarde*

A
1. *Pied en l'air droit.* } *Fleuret.*
2. *Pied en l'air gauche.* }
3. *Grue droite.* }
4. *Pied en l'air gauche.* } *Fleuret.*
5. *Pied en l'air droit.* }
6. *Grue gauche.* }
7. *Saut majeur.*
8. *Posture droite.*

Reverse.

B
1. *Pied en l'air gauche.* } *Fleuret.*
2. *Pied en l'air droit.* }
3. *Grue gauche.* }
4. *Pied en l'air droit.* } *Fleuret.*
5. *Pied en l'air gauche.* }
6. *Grue droite.* }
7. *Saut majeur.*
8. *Posture gauche.*

I was lately present at a wedding where I saw a young man executing a Five Steps which, too, seemed very graceful. He danced it in this way :—

Air of the *Gaillarde* called *La Fatigue*

Another series of movements to be made by the dancer in performing this *Gaillarde*

A
1. *Posture gauche.*
2. *Grue gauche.*
3. Turn the body to the left side, then contrariwise, and make a *grue droite.*
4. *Grue gauche.*
5. *Saut majeur.*
6. *Posture droite.*

Reverse.

B
1. *Posture droite.*
2. *Grue droite.*
3. Turn the body to the right side, then contrariwise, and make a *grue gauche.*
4. *Grue droite.*
5. *Saut majeur.*
6. *Posture droite.*

And thus continue by repeating from the beginning.

You will note that these Five Steps will gain in grace if you do them mincingly.

Capriol. What do you mean by " mincingly " ?

Arbeau. You make mincing steps when you convert the five crotchets to ten quavers, and instead of making one step with its *petit saut* at the same moment, you will make it in two parts, carrying forward the *petit saut* to the first quaver beat, and immediately after making the step on the second quaver beat. And such kinds of mincing steps actually make no more than five ordinary steps, but they are more graceful and less heavy, for, instead of coming to the ground all at once, you do so gradually.

Capriol. If it should happen that the music consisted only of crotchets could the *fleurets* be adapted to it ?

Arbeau. Yes, certainly, for imagining the last crotchet to be divided into two quavers, of the first two steps you would make three. And you would do likewise with the third crotchet, so that your phrase would contain seven steps and movements, as if the music were noted in this way, and thus you will make such divisions as please you, and set more or less steps to the music as you see fit.

Capriol. The *saut majeur* and the *posture* take the time of two crotchets. In making two quavers of the rest, I could then make another *fleuret*, and thus the two bars in triple time would be covered by three *fleurets*.

Arbeau. You are right. But there would be no cadence at all, and you must make the cadence on the fourth bar, and that would be called making a passage, because you would omit a cadence to introduce it later on. And, supposing you made two *fleurets* and one *posture* to the two bars following, your passage would contain sixteen steps in all, that is to say, nine steps for the first three *fleurets* and seven steps for the two *fleurets*, *saut majeur* and *posture* of the cadence, sixteen steps in all. And if you still wished to pass over and defer your cadence until the sixth bar of triple time, your passage would contain twenty-five steps and movements.

Capriol. You told me above that the first passage after the Five Steps is completed in the fourth bar with eleven steps, and in the sixth bar with seventeen steps, and in the eighth with twenty-three ; and so you count six steps for the two bars where one omits and five for the two bars where one performs the cadence.

Arbeau. I did tell you so. But that is when one step is danced to each crotchet. Now the number of steps is augmented, when we divide a crotchet into two quavers and to each quaver we desire to assign a step. Also, when the passages are less than eleven, seventeen or twenty-three steps, and when we make use of two or three crotchets to a single step, you will remember what I have told you, that the dancer's action is beautiful only when the movements of the feet keep time with the beats of music ; as you will find out in the air of the *Gaillarde* called *La Milanaise*, which, as you will see below, is composed of a passage of eleven steps extended to fifteen by five *fleurets* followed by a Five Steps shortened to three.

Capriol. Can *fleurets* be executed in dancing the *Gaillarde* when the music does not contain a crotchet divided into two quavers?

Arbeau. Easily, by imagining this sub-division, even when it is not so noted. And, generally, you could, whether in writing or in imagination, make your bars of whole or divided notes as you please.

Capriol. I await the air of this *Milanaise* and the tabulation of the steps and movements which can be adapted to it.

Air of the *Gaillarde* called *La Milanaise*

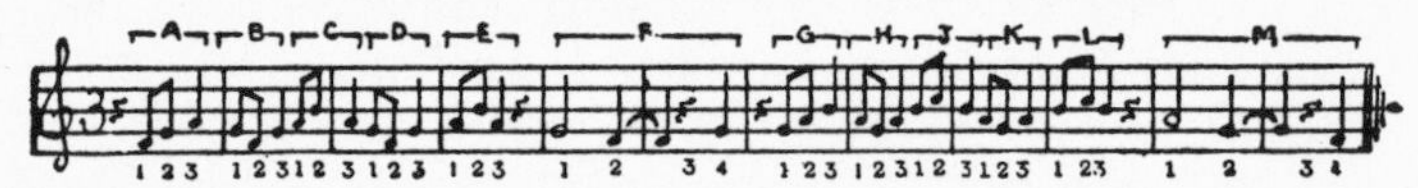

Movements to be made by the dancer in performing this *Gaillarde*

A
1. *Pied en l'air droit*, without a *petit saut*.
2. *Pied en l'air gauche*, without a *petit saut*.
3. *Grue droite*.

} *Fleuret*.

B
1. *Pied en l'air gauche*, without a *petit saut*.
2. *Pied en l'air droit*, without a *petit saut*.
3. *Grue gauche*.

} *Fleuret*.

C
1. *Pied en l'air droit*, without a *petit saut*.
2. *Pied en l'air gauche*, without a *petit saut*.
3. *Grue droite*.

} *Fleuret*.

D
1. *Pied en l'air gauche*, without a *petit saut*.
2. *Pied en l'air droit*, without a *petit saut*.
3. *Grue gauche*.

} *Fleuret*.

E
1. *Pied en l'air droit*, without a *petit saut*.
2. *Pied en l'air gauche*, without a *petit saut*.
3. *Grue droite*.

} *Fleuret*.

F
1. *Pied croisé droit*, without a *petit saut*.
2. *Révérence passagière droite*, or *entretaille droite* making a *grue gauche*.
3. *Saut majeur*.
4. *Posture droite*.

Reverse.

G
1. *Pied en l'air gauche*, without a *petit saut*.
2. *Pied en l'air droit*, without a *petit saut*.
3. *Grue gauche*.
} *Fleuret*.

H
1. *Pied in l'air droit*, without a *petit saut*.
2. *Pied en l'air gauche*, without a *petit saut*.
3. *Grue droite*.
} *Fleuret*.

J
1. *Pied en l'air gauche*, without a *petit saut*.
2. *Pied en l'air droit*, without a *petit saut*.
3. *Grue gauche*.
} *Fleuret*.

K
1. *Pied en l'air droit*, without a *petit saut*.
2. *Pied en l'air gauche*, without a *petit saut*.
3. *Grue droite*.
} *Fleuret*.

L
1. *Pied en l'air gauche*, without a *petit saut*.
2. *Pied en l'air droit*, without a *petit saut*.
3. *Grue gauche*.
} *Fleuret*.

M
1. *Pied croisé gauche*.
2. *Révérence passagière gauche*, or *entretaille gauche* making a *grue droite*.
3. *Saut majeur*.
4. *Posture gauche*.

And continue thus by repeating from the beginning.

Capriol. Let us dismiss this; give me the tabulation of some passage of eleven steps.

Arbeau. Passages of eleven steps can be made by linking or joining together two phrases of five steps, or such equivalents as you may choose ; provided that in place of the rest, on which is made the *saut majeur* of the first phrase, you add a movement to it or convert the rest and the *posture* following into a *fleuret* or two steps, so as to interrupt this first cadence. And if you do not wish to take this trouble, you will aid yourself by the following tabulation until such time as you may learn others from some good dancers, because practice will teach you more than precepts. And you will observe that these passages of eleven or more steps are naturally adapted for the conclusion of *Gaillardes*, and will exhibit a better grace when they are done by turning the body.

Air of the *Gaillarde* called *J'aymerois mieulx dormir seulette &c.*

Movements to be made by the dancer in executing this *Gaillarde*

A
1. *Ruade droite.*
2. *Entretaille* making a *grue gauche.*
3. *Ruade gauche.*
4. *Grue gauche.*
5. *Ruade droite.*
6. *Entretaille* making a *grue gauche.*

B
1. *Ruade gauche.*
2. *Entretaille* making a *grue droite.*
3. *Ruade droite.*
4. *Entretaille* making a *grue gauche.*
5. *Saut majeur* in preparation for the *cadence.*
6. *Cadence* in *posture droite.*

Reverse of the preceding passage.

C
1. *Ruade gauche.*
2. *Entretaille* making a *grue droite.*
3. *Ruade droite.*
4. *Grue droite.*
5. *Ruade gauche.*
6. *Entretaille* making a *grue droite.*

D
1. *Ruade droite.*
2. *Entretaille* making a *grue gauche.*
3. *Ruade gauche.*
4. *Entretaille* making a *grue droite.*
5. *Saut majeur* in preparation for the *cadence.*
6. *Cadence* in *posture gauche.*

You must turn the body twice in dancing the eleven steps, and as many times when dancing the reverse, for a single turn of the body would not suffice.

Another passage of eleven steps

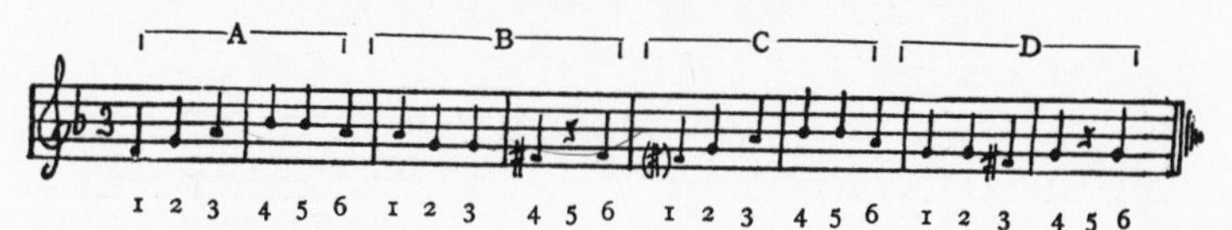

A
1. *Ruade gauche.*
2. *Grue gauche.*
3. *Ruade gauche.*
4. *Grue gauche.*
5. *Posture droite.*
6. *Grue droite.*

B
1. *Posture gauche.*
2. *Grue gauche.*
3. *Ruade gauche.*
4. *Grue gauche.*
5. *Saut majeur* in preparation for the *cadence.*
6. *Cadence* in *posture droite.*

Reverse of the preceding passage.

C
1. *Ruade droite.*
2. *Grue droite.*
3. *Ruade droite.*
4. *Grue droite.*
5. *Posture gauche.*
6. *Grue gauche.*

D
1. *Posture droite.*
2. *Grue droite.*
3. *Ruade droite.*
4. *Grue droite.*
5. *Saut majeur* in preparation for the cadence.
6. *Cadence* in *posture gauche.*

Air of the *Gaillarde* called *L'ennuy qui me tormente &c.*

(Another passage of eleven steps)

Movements to be made by the dancer in performing this *Gaillarde*

A
1. *Grue droite.*
2. *Grue droite.*
3. *Ruade gauche.*
4. *Grue gauche.*
5. *Posture droite.*
6. *Grue droite.*

B
1. *Posture gauche.*
2. *Grue gauche.*
3. *Ruade gauche.*
4. *Grue gauche.*
5. *Saut majeur* in preparation for the *cadence.*
6. *Cadence* in *posture droite.*

Reverse of the preceding passage.

C
1. *Grue gauche.*
2. *Grue gauche.*
3. *Ruade droite.*
4. *Grue droite.*
5. *Posture gauche.*
6. *Grue gauche.*

D
1. *Posture droite.*
2. *Grue droite.*
3. *Ruade droite.*
4. *Grue droite.*
5. *Saut majeur.*
6. *Posture gauche.*

Capriol. I have, thanks be to God, enough knowledge now to practise the *Gaillarde.* All the same, I pray you give me a further couple of passages if it does not weary you.

Another passage of eleven steps

E
1. *Ruade droite.*
2. *Entretaille* making a *grue gauche.*
3. *Ruade droite.*
4. *Entretaille* making a *grue gauche.*
5. *Posture droite.*
6. *Grue droite.*

F
1. *Posture gauche.*
2. *Grue gauche.*
3. *Ruade gauche.*
4. *Grue gauche.*
5. *Saut majeur.*
6. *Posture droite.*

Reverse of the preceding passage.

G
1. *Ruade gauche.*
2. *Entretaille* making a *grue droite.*
3. *Ruade gauche.*
4. *Entretaille* making a *grue droite.*
5. *Posture gauche.*
6. *Grue gauche.*

H
1. *Posture droite.*
2. *Grue droite.*
3. *Ruade droite.*
4. *Grue droite.*
5. *Saut majeur.*
6. *Posture gauche.*

Another passage of eleven steps where the sixth step is divided into two, and the seventh likewise, so that there are thirteen steps in place of eleven.

A

1. *Pieds joints.*
2. *Grue droite.*
3. *Entretaille* making a *grue gauche.*
4. *Entretaille* making a *grue droite.*
5. *Posture droite.*
6. *Grue gauche.*
7. *Posture droite.*
8. *Grue droite.*
9. *Posture gauche.*
10. *Grue droite.*
11. *Grue droite.*
12. *Grue droite.*
13. *Saut majeur.*
14. *Posture gauche.*

Reverse of the preceding passage.

B

1. *Pieds joints.*
2. *Grue gauche.*
3. *Entretaille* making a *grue droite.*
4. *Entretaille* making a *grue gauche.*
5. *Posture gauche.*
6. *Grue droite.*
7. *Posture gauche.*
8. *Grue gauche.*
9. *Posture droite.*
10. *Grue gauche.*
11. *Grue gauche.*
12. *Grue gauche.*
13. *Saut majeur.*
14. *Posture droite.*

Arbeau. To make passages of seventeen steps you must link together three phrases of five steps and interrupt the first two at the cadence. Or else link together a passage of eleven steps with a phrase of five, and interrupt all the cadences except the last. To make passages of twenty-three steps you must link together four phrases of five steps or two passages of eleven steps, and interrupt all the cadences except the last. And so on in like manner.

Capriol. That is very easy; see if I do not perform the first passage of eleven steps properly.

Arbeau. You have executed your steps and movements well and fallen properly into cadence, but when you dance in company never look down to examine your steps and ascertain if you dance them correctly. Hold your head and body upright with a confident mien, and do not spit or blow your nose much. And if necessity obliges you to do so, turn your head away and use a fair white handkerchief. Converse pleasantly in a low and modest voice, let your arms fall by your sides neither in a lifeless nor in a restless manner, and be suitably and neatly dressed, your hose well drawn up and your shoes clean. And bear these counsels in mind, not only in dancing the *Gaillarde*, but in performing all other kinds of dances.

We have discoursed of the *Gaillarde* enough, so that there is no advantage to be gained in pursuing the subject except to tell you that you now understand it is easy to divide the *double* of a *Pavane* by extending it with such movements as you choose. These will be measured by six crotchets, a rest for the *saut majeur*, and a *posture*, or similarly by twelve quavers, a rest for the *saut majeur*, and a *posture ;* or, by extensions and abridgments of their combinations, each containing the same measure of time which we should take for performing the *double* which you wish to divide. There are some persons so agile and such high leapers that they have devised many *sauts*, and sometimes doubled or trebled these *sauts* instead of performing the five or eleven steps, and at the conclusion of the *sauts* have come to the ground at the cadence so neatly that they have acquired the reputation of being very fine dancers. But it sometimes happens that in making these agile *sauts* they fall down, and the raillery and laughter occasioned have made them take to flight. Hence the best teachers have always advised that these *sauts* should not be made, or else performed so easily that the dancer should not fall into such straits.

Capriol. This is now quite clear to me. For the rest, I

should be well content not to pass over the *Volte*, since it is coming into fashion.

LA VOLTE

Arbeau. The *Volte*[1] is a kind of *Gaillarde* familiar to the people of Provence, which, like the *tordion*, is danced in triple time. The movements and steps of this dance are made while turning the body, and consist of two steps, a rest for the *saut majeur*, a *pieds joints*, and lastly, two rests or pauses. To understand the above, let us suppose that you are facing me in the position *pieds joints*. For the first step, make a fairly short *pied en l'air* while springing on your left foot, and at the same time, turn your left shoulder towards me. Then, for the second, make a fairly long step with your right foot, without springing, and while doing so, turn your back to me. Then make the *saut majeur* while turning your body and fall into the position *pieds joints*, at the same time turning your right shoulder towards me. So the first turn is accomplished.

Capriol. According to your teaching the body is not completely turned.

Arbeau. If one were to turn the body completely, one would find oneself in the same position as at the beginning, and would hardly have moved at all from one's original position. After the first turn, in which the body moves three-quarters of the way round, you will make the second turn with a short *pied en l'air* for the first step, as before, while springing on your left foot, and at the same time turn facing me. Then, for the second step, take a fairly long step on your right foot without jumping, and in doing so turn your left shoulder towards me. Then make the *saut majeur* while turning your body, and fall into the position *pieds joints*, at the same time turning your back to me.

For the third turn and cadence make a fairly short *pied en l'air* for the first step while springing on your left foot, turning your right side to me at the same time. Then, for the second step, take a fairly long step on your right foot, without jumping, and at the same time turn facing me. Then make the *saut majeur* while turning your body, fall into the position *pieds joints*, and at the same time turn your left shoulder towards me. For the fourth turn and cadence,

[1] Literally *a turning round.*

take a fairly short *pied en l'air* for the first step, while springing on your left foot, and at the same time turn your back to me. Then take a fairly long step on your right foot, without jumping, and at the same time turn your right shoulder towards me. Then make the *saut majeur* while turning your body, fall into the position *pieds joints*, and at the same time turn facing me so that you come into the same position as at the beginning. And so you see that in four cadences you can return to the same place and position as you were in at the beginning. All the same, I do not make this a fixed rule, because it may happen that you will turn quicker or slower. But I have described a hypothetical case to make it clearer to you.

Capriol. If I hold the damsel by the hand it would be impossible for her to make the turn with me, because she is farther away from the centre.

Arbeau. Your argument is a good one, supposing, as you must, that the damsel makes the same steps and movements as you. And, on this account, the dancer of the *Volte*, regarding himself as the centre of a circle, should bring the damsel as near as possible to him when he wishes to turn, since, by this means, she will find the steps smaller and easier to perform. You will bring her near to you in the following manner:

Make your *révérence* (holding the damsel by the hand), and before turning, perform some steps about the room by way of preparation, as if you were dancing the *tordion*. Now observe that some people dance this beginning by making five steps to the right and five to the left alternately, or better, by making five steps reduced to two steps, a *saut majeur* and a *posture*, and the same for the reverse movement, and so on. Others dance this beginning like the rest of the *Volte* by a *pied en l'air*, a step, a *saut majeur* and a *pieds joints*, as explained above.

Capriol. Which kind do you favour the more?

Arbeau. The last kind, because, by this means, this dance becomes uniform in all its parts, as much at the beginning as at the end. When you wish to turn, let go of the damsel's left hand and throw your left arm round her back, seizing and clasping her about the waist. At the same time throw your right hand below her bust to help her to spring when you push her before you with your left thigh. She, on her part, will place her right hand on your back or collar, and her left on her thigh, to hold her petticoat or kirtle in place, lest the breeze caused by the movement should reveal her chemise or her naked thigh. This accomplished, you execute together the turns of the *Volte* described above. After having turned for as many cadences as it pleases you, restore the damsel to her place, when she will feel, whatever good face she puts upon it, her brain confused, her head full of giddy whirlings, and you cannot feel in much better case. I leave you to consider if it be a proper thing for a young girl to make such large steps and separations of the legs; and whether in the *Volte* both honour and health are not concerned and threatened. I have already given you my opinion of the matter.

Capriol. These swimmings and whirlings of the head would distress me.

Arbeau. Then dance some other kind of dance. Or, if you dance this to the left, begin again the next time to the right, and thus, the second time, turn contrariwise to the way you turned the first time.

Air of a *Volte*

Movements to be made by the dancers in performing the *Volte*

A
1. Spring a little distance forward on the left foot, at the same time execute a *pied en l'air droit*.
2. Take a fairly long step on the right foot.
3. *Saut majeur*.
4. Come to the ground in the position *pieds joints*.

B
1. Spring a little distance forward on the left foot, at the same time execute a *pied en l'air droit*.
2. Take a fairly long step on the right foot.
3. *Saut majeur*.
4. Come to the ground in the position *pieds joints*.

C
1. Spring a little distance forward on the left foot, at the same time execute a *pied en l'air droit*.
2. Take a fairly long step on the right foot.
3. *Saut majeur*.
4. Come to the ground in the position *pieds joints*.

D
1. Spring a little distance forward on the left foot, at the same time execute a *pied en l'air droit*.
2. Take a fairly long step on the right foot.
3. *Saut majeur*.
4. Come to the ground in the position *pieds joints*.

You will continue to turn by cadences to the left, as often as it pleases you. And if another time you wish to dance the *Volte* turning to the right, you should place your right hand on the damsel's back and the left below her bust, and, pushing her with your right thigh beneath her rump, turn her in the reverse direction to that shown in the tabulation above. And mark that it requires dexterity to seize and clasp the damsel to you, for this must be accomplished in two bars of triple time ; so that, on the first bar, you take a step to place yourself in front of her, at the end of the second you have one hand on her hip and the other below her bust, and are ready, by the third bar, to begin to turn according to the steps contained in the tabulation.

Capriol. How should the *Courante* be danced ? Is it very different from the *Volte ?*

LA COURANTE

Arbeau. It differs considerably from the *Volte*, and is danced to a light duple time, consisting of two *simples* and a *double* to the left, and the same to the right, going forwards or sideways and sometimes backwards as it pleases the dancer. And note that the steps of the *Courante* [1] must be *sauté*,[2] which is not done in the *Pavane* or in the *Basse-Danse*. To make a *simple à gauche* [3] in the *Courante*, you, having assumed a proper bearing, will spring off the right foot and

[1] This dance originated from Italy and derived its name of *Corrente* (stream) from the manner of its short advances and retreats, and flexible movements of the knees, reminiscent of the movements of a fish when it lightly dives below the surface of the water to come again to the surface. *Vide :* Laure Fonta, *Notice sur les danses du XVIe siècle.* (This prefaces the reprint of Arbeau's *Orchésographie*, published in 1888.)

[2] Literally *jumped*.

[3] Literally *single to the left*.

come to the ground on the left foot for your first step, then spring off the right, at the same time falling into *pieds joints* for the second step, and thus the *simple à gauche* will be accomplished. Do the same in the reverse manner for the *simple à droite*.[1] For the *double à gauche*,[2] spring off the right foot, coming to the ground on the left foot for the first step, then spring off the left foot, making the second step with the right foot, then spring off the right foot, making the third step with the left foot. Then spring off the right foot, making the fourth step and fall into the position *pieds joints*. And thus the *double à gauche* will be accomplished. Do the same in the reverse manner for the two *simples*, and a *double à droite*.

In my young days there was a kind of game and ballet arranged to the *Courante*. For three young men would choose three girls, and having placed themselves in a row, the first dancer would lead his damsel to the end of the room, when he would return alone to his companions. The second would do the same, then the third, so that the three girls were left by themselves at one end of the room and three young men at the other. And when the third had returned, the first, gambolling and making all manner of amorous glances, pulling his hose tight and setting his shirt straight, went to claim his damsel, who refused his arm and turned her back upon him; then, seeing the young manhad returned to his place, she pretended to be in despair. The two others did the same. At last all three went together to claim their respective damsels, and kneeling on the ground, begged this boon with clasped hands, when the damsels fell into their arms and all danced the *Courante* pell-mell.

Capriol. Are *Courantes* still danced after this same fashion ?

Arbeau. As for the steps, they should be the same. But young men who do not know and have never learned what a *simple* is nor a *double* either, dance it according to their fancy, and are content simply to keep time in the cadence ; and, in dancing it, they turn the body, letting go of the damsel's hand. After the turn is done, still dancing, they again take their damsels by the hand and continue. And when any man is observed by his companions to be tired, they go and steal his damsel and lead her away to dance ; or, if they see

[1] Literally *single to the right*. [2] Literally *double to the left*.

that his first partner is weary, they provide him with another. Here is a tabulation of the *Courante.*

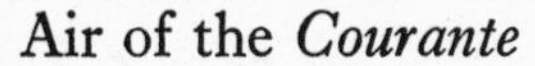

Air of the *Courante*

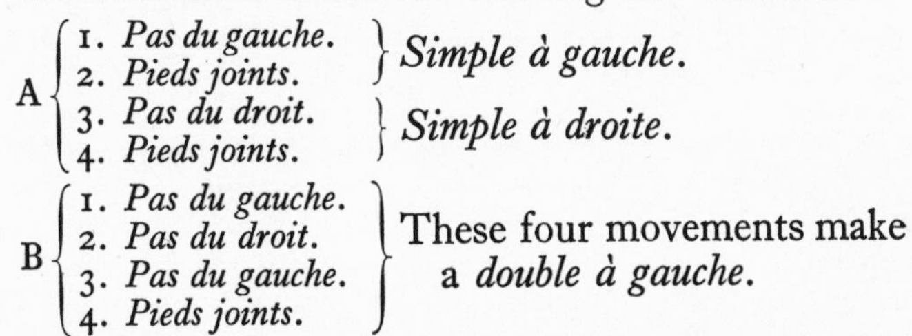

Movements suitable for dancing the *Courante*

A	1. *Pas du gauche.*	*Simple à gauche.*
	2. *Pieds joints.*	
	3. *Pas du droit.*	*Simple à droite.*
	4. *Pieds joints.*	
B	1. *Pas du gauche.*	These four movements make a *double à gauche.*
	2. *Pas du droit.*	
	3. *Pas du gauche.*	
	4. *Pieds joints.*	

You do the same thing for the reverse and continue by repeating the beginning. None of the crotchet-beats in the tabulation above are empty, and on each beat you will make a *petit saut* to accompany the movement, or when you are tired, and do not wish to jump, you may treat some of them as rests.

Capriol. What is the dance called the *Allemande?*

L'ALLEMANDE

Arbeau. The *Allemande* is a plain dance of a certain gravity, familiar to the Germans, and, I believe, is one of our most ancient dances, for we are descended from the Germans. You can dance it in company. For, having taken a damsel by the hand, several others can take up their position behind you, each with his partner, and you dance together in duple time, going forward, or backward if you wish, three steps and a *grue*, or a *pied en l'air* without a *saut*, and in some cases by a step and a *grue* or a *pied en l'air.* And when you have arrived at the end of the room, you can dance while turning round, without loosing hold of your damsel. The other dancers who will follow you do the same until they arrive at the end of the room. And when the musicians finish the first part, each dancer stops and converses with his damsel;

and you begin again as before for the second part. And when you come to the third part, you will dance it in the same duple time, but with greater lightness and animation, and with the same steps, only adding *petits sauts* to them, as in the *Courante*. This you will easily understand from the tabulation, which is hardly necessary, since there is little variety of movement ; all the same, in order that you may see the whole as clearly as possible, I have not spared myself the trouble of giving it to you in writing.

Air of the first and second parts of the *Allemande*

Movements to be made in dancing the *Allemande*

A
1. *Pas du gauche.*
2. *Pas du droit.*
3. *Pas du gauche.*
4. *Grue droite.*

B
1. *Pas du droit.*
2. *Pas du gauche.*
3. *Pas du droit.*
4. *Grue gauche.*

C
1. *Pas du gauche.*
2. *Pas du droit.*
3. *Pas du gauche.*
4. *Grue droite.*

D
1. *Pas du droit.*
2. *Pas du gauche.*
3. *Pas du droit.*
4. *Grue gauche.*

E
1. *Pas du gauche.*
2. *Grue droite.*
3. *Pas du droit.*
4. *Grue gauche.*

Continuation of the Air

Continuation of the movements of the *Allemande*

F
1. *Pas du gauche.*
2. *Pas du droit.*
3. *Pas du gauche.*
4. *Grue droite.*

G
1. *Pas du droit.*
2. *Pas du gauche.*
3. *Pas du droit.*
4. *Grue gauche.*

Tabulation of the third part of the *Allemande* which is danced in duple time, like the *Courante*, with these movements

1. *Pas du gauche.*
2. *Pas du droit.*
3. *Pas du gauche.*
4. *Grue droite.*

Reverse.

5. *Pas du droit.*
6. *Pas du gauche.*
7. *Pas du droit.*
8. *Grue gauche.*

And continue thus by repeating from the beginning.

The crotchets, which are here empty, take the place of rests and pauses, or *petits sauts*, as has been said of the *Courante*. In dancing the *Allemande*, a young man may sometimes steal a damsel, taking her from her partner; and the one who is thus robbed endeavours to capture another's. But I do not approve at all of this manner of dancing it, since it may lead to quarrels and discontent.

Capriol. I am told that in good society the dance is generally opened by *Branles*. Tell me how they are danced.

BRANLE DOUBLE

Arbeau. Since you are well aware how to dance the *Pavane* and the *Basse-Danse*, it will be easy for you to dance *Branles* in the same duple time, and you must know that in *Branles* the dancers move sideways and not forward. In the first place, regarding the *Branle* called *Branle Double*, you will make a *double à gauche*, then a *double à droite*. You already know that a *double* consists of three steps and a *pieds joints*. To make these sideways, you will assume a proper bearing after the *révérence* of salutation and, holding the right foot firm, fling the left foot out sideways, which will make a *pieds largis* for the first bar. Then, for the second bar, holding the left foot firm, bring the right foot near the left, which will make a *demi-pieds joints*. For the third bar, holding the right foot firm, fling the left foot out sideways, which will make a *pieds largis*. And for the fourth bar, holding the left foot firm, bring the right foot up to the left, which will make a *pieds joints*. These four steps made in four bars or drum-rhythms we will call a *double à gauche ;* and you will make a *double à droite* in the reverse manner: that is, holding yourself firm and standing on the left foot, fling the right foot out sideways, which will make a *pieds largis* for the fifth bar. Then, for the sixth bar, holding the right foot firm, bring the left foot near the right, which will make a *demi-pieds joints*. For the seventh bar, holding the left foot firm, fling the right foot out sideways, which will make a *pieds largis*. Finally, for the eighth bar, holding the right foot firm, bring the left foot up to the right in a *pieds joints*, and these last four steps we will call a *double à droite*. And thus, in these eight steps and bars, the *Branle Double* will be completed, as you see in the tabulation, and you will repeat as at the beginning, making a *double à gauche*, then a *double à droite*.

Capriol. I hear down in your little room Master Guillaume with his viol. Give me the tabulation for the *Branle Double*, and I will practise it to see if I succeed in performing it.

Arbeau. This is very timely. Let us go down and make him play his viol. Musicians are accustomed to begin the dances at a festival by a *Branle Double*, which is called *Branle Commun*, and afterwards they give the *Branle Simple*, then the *Branle Gai*, and at the end the *Branles* which are called *Branles de Bourgogne*, and others which some call *Branles de Champagne*. The order of these four kinds of *Branles* is governed by the three types of people who take part in a dance. The old people gravely dance the *Branles Doubles* and *Branles Simples*, the young married ones dance the *Branles Gais*, and the youngest of all dance the *Branles de Bourgogne*. And all those who take part in the dance acquit themselves as best they can, each according to his age, disposition and agility.

Tabulation for dancing *Branles Doubles*

Air of a *Branle Double*

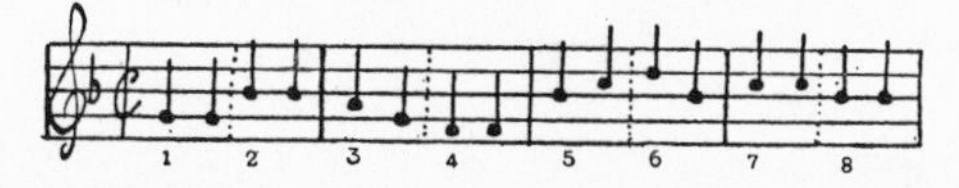

Movements for dancing the *Branle Double*

1. *Pied largi gauche.* 2. *Pied droit approché.* 3. *Pied largi gauche.* 4. *Pied droit joint.*	These four steps make a *double à gauche.*
5. *Pied largi droit.* 6. *Pied gauche approché.* 7. *Pied largi droit.* 8. *Pied gauche joint.*	These four steps make a *double à droite.*

Capriol. This *Branle Double* is very easy to dance, but it seems to me that the dancers do not move from one place, since they make four steps to the left, and then four to the right.

Arbeau. To counteract that, they make the *double à droite* shorter, and thus always move slowly to the left. In other cases, in place of the *double à droite*, they make a *reprise* or a *branle*.

Capriol. The *Branles* please me because many can delight in them together.

Arbeau. When you have commenced a *Branle*, many others will join you, both young men and damsels. And sometimes, the damsel who is the last comer will take your left hand and thus make a round dance.

Capriol. When there is no round dance, does the one who leads the dance always remain the first ?

Arbeau. Yes, usually, for no other could be found who, with his damsel, would presume to take the lead, even if he were a nobleman of renown whom one would not wish to cross.

Capriol. What place will be taken by him who wishes to join in the dance ?

Arbeau. He will place himself at the end, holding his damsel by her right hand, or else will, if permitted, take a place between those who are dancing.

Capriol. Are there no divisions in dancing these *Branles ?*

Arbeau. It has always been held that the more gravely and slowly the *Branles Doubles* are danced, the better they are. All the same, it is not improper to make a *pied en l'air gauche* on the first crotchet of the seventh bar, and a *pied en l'air droit* on the second crotchet of the seventh bar ; and on the first crotchet of the eighth and last bar, a *pied en l'air gauche* ready to continue and repeat the beginning, holding the left foot in the air for the time of the last crotchet.

Continuation of the Air of a *Branle Double*

Divided movements as explained above

1. *Pied largi gauche.* 2. *Pied droit approché.* 3. *Pied largi gauche.* 4. *Pied droit joint.*	These four steps make a *double à gauche.*
5. *Pied largi droit.* 6. *Pied gauche approché.* 7. *Pied en l'air gauche.* 8. *Pied en l'air droit.* 9. *Pied en l'air gauche.*	These five steps make a *double à droite decoupé.*
10. Rest.	

Capriol. Are there no divisions made in *Branles Doubles?*

Arbeau. Young men who have an excess of agility make these divisions at their pleasure. But I counsel you to dance them sedately.

BRANLE SIMPLE

According to the same duple time, and by the same steps which I gave you for the *Branle Double*, you can dance the *Branle Simple*, making a *double à gauche* for the beginning. But here is the difference between them; for, instead of making after this a *double à droite*, you will only execute a *simple* by making a *pieds largis* with the right foot, and for the conclusion a *pieds joints* with the left foot. You may divide the last four crotchets of this *simple* into three *pieds en l'air* and a rest, as I said just now when speaking of the *Branle Double*.

Tabulation of the *Branle Simple*

Air of a *Branle Simple*

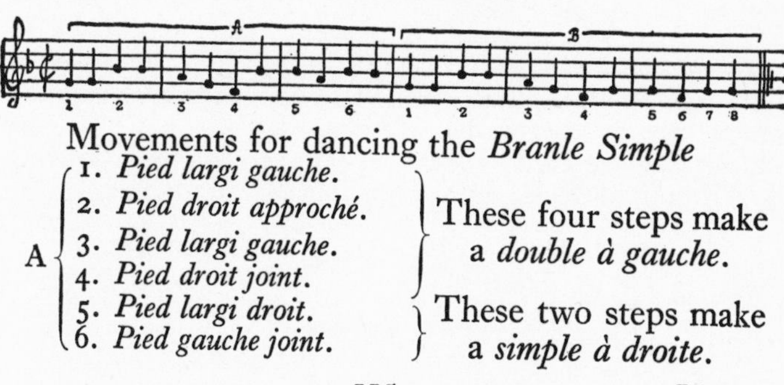

Movements for dancing the *Branle Simple*

A	1. *Pied largi gauche.* 2. *Pied droit approché.* 3. *Pied largi gauche.* 4. *Pied droit joint.*	These four steps make a *double à gauche.*
	5. *Pied largi droit.* 6. *Pied gauche joint.*	These two steps make a *simple à droite.*

B
1. *Pied largi gauche.*
2. *Pied droit approché.*
3. *Pied largi gauche.*
4. *Pied droit joint.*

These four steps made a *double à gauche.*

5. *Pied en l'air gauche.*
6. *Pied en l'air droit.*
7. *Pied en l'air gauche.*

These three steps make a *simple à droite.*

8. Rest.

BRANLE GAI

After the *Branle Simple* comes the *Branle Gai*, which you will dance in two bars of triple time to the left only, in four steps and a pause. To do this, step sideways on the left foot and execute a *pied en l'air droit* for the first step on the first crotchet. Then bring the right foot up to the left, and, placing it on the ground, execute a *pied en l'air gauche* for the second step on the second crotchet. Then step sideways on the left foot and execute a *pied en l'air droit* for the third step on the third crotchet; then bring the right foot close up to the left, and, placing it on the ground, execute a *pied en l'air gauche*, and keep the foot thus, ready to repeat the beginning, for the time of two crotchets, which will be equal to two rests or a pause. And if you find minims in the tabulation, imagine them to be divided into crotchets to suit the steps according to the manner of dancing the *Branle Gai*.

Tabulation of the *Branle Gai*

Air of the *Branle Gai*

Movements suitable for dancing this *Branle*

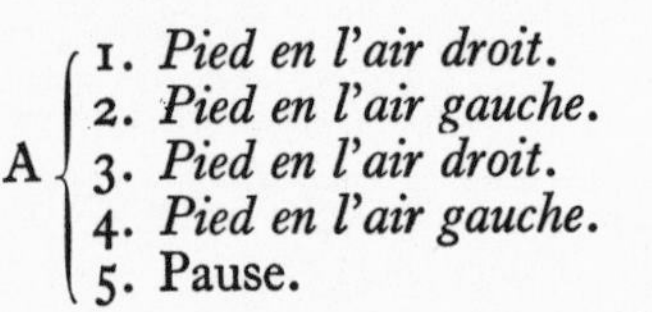
A
1. *Pied en l'air droit.*
2. *Pied en l'air gauche.*
3. *Pied en l'air droit.*
4. *Pied en l'air gauche.*
5. Pause.

B
1. *Pied en l'air droit.*
2. *Pied en l'air gauche.*
3. *Pied en l'air droit.*
4. *Pied en l'air gauche.*
5. Pause.

C
1. *Pied en l'air droit.*
2. *Pied en l'air gauche.*
3. *Pied en l'air droit.*
4. *Pied en l'air gauche.*
5. Pause.

D
1. *Pied en l'air droit.*
2. *Pied en l'air gauche.*
3. *Pied en l'air droit.*
4. *Pied en l'air gauche.*
5. Pause.

Capriol. This *Branle* is rightly called gay, because, as I understand it, one foot is always in the air. But continue, and tell me of the *Branle* which you call *Branle de Bourgogne.*

BRANLE DE BOURGOGNE

Arbeau. After the *Branle Gai*, the musicians play the *Branle de Bourgogne*, which is danced from side to side in duple time, using the same steps as the *Branle Double*, but the time of this *Branle* is lighter and more animated. There is no difference in the steps, save that, in place of *pieds joints*, *grues* or *pieds en l'air* are executed for the fourth and eighth steps.

Tabulation of the *Branle de Bourgogne*

Air of the *Branle de Bourgogne*

Movements suitable for dancing this *Branle*

1. *Pied largi gauche.*
2. *Pied droit approché.*
3. *Pied largi gauche.*
4. *Grue droite*, or *pied en l'air.*

These four steps make a *double à gauche.*

5. *Pied largi droit.* 6. *Pied gauche approché.* 7. *Pied largi droit.* 8. *Grue gauche*, or *pied en l'air.*	These four steps make a *double à droite.*

And you will continue thus by repeating from the beginning.

BRANLE DU HAUT BARROIS

There is another kind of *Branle* called the *Haut Barrois*,[1] which is danced like the *Branle Double* or the *Branle de Bourgogne*. But this *Branle* is different, since it not only demands movements of the feet, but requires the movement of the shoulders and arms, with *petits sauts*, in light and animated duple time. To dance it, spring sideways on both feet to the left, falling into the position *pied largi gauche*. Then spring sideways again on both feet to the left, falling in the position *pied droit approché ;* then spring sideways to the left, falling into the position *pied largi gauche*. Then again spring sideways on both feet to the left, falling into the position *pieds joints ;* or better, falling on the left foot and making a *grue droite ;* or, better still, a *pied en l'air droit*, and thus the *double à gauche* will be completed. Do the same in the reverse manner to the right to execute a *double à droite*. And if the air of the *Branle du Haut Barrois* is like the *Branle Simple*, you will cut off the two penultimate bars to complete the *simple*. This *Branle* is danced by serving men and wenches, and sometimes by young men and damsels of gentle birth when they make a masquerade disguised as peasants and shepherds, or when they dance merrily among themselves. The tabulation of the *Branle Double* and *Branle Simple* set down above should suffice you, so I shall give you one of them arranged to the air of *Monstierandel*.

Capriol. This *Branle* seems to me more stirring than the preceding ones, and should be good to dance in winter to make oneself warm. Since you have begun giving me tabulations, I pray you give me that of this particular *Branle*.

[1] *Barrois* is the country round Bar-le-Duc.

Tabulation of the *Branle du Haut Barrois*

Air of the *Branle du Haut Barrois*

Movements for dancing the *Branle du Haut Barrois*

A
1. *Pied largi gauche.*
2. *Petit saut.*
3. *Pied droit approché.*
4. *Petit saut.*
5. *Pied largi gauche.*
6. *Petit saut.*
7. *Pieds joints.*
8. *Petit saut.*

These four steps make a *double à gauche.*

B
1. *Pied largi droit.*
2. *Petit saut.*
3. *Pied gauche approché.*
4. *Petit saut.*
5. *Pied largi droit.*
6. *Petit saut.*
7. *Pieds joints.*
8. *Petit saut.*

And you will continue thus by repeating from the beginning.

The various *Branles* described already are the source from which are derived certain other *Branles* composed of a medley of *doubles*, *simples*, *pieds en l'air*, *pieds joints* and *sauts*, sometimes varied by the insertion of various slow or quick bars accordingly as it pleases the composers and inventors. Musicians call them *Branles de Champagne coupés*.

And so as to group these together they have arranged these *Branles* in a series of certain numbers, like our Langres musicians, who always play ten in succession, which they call *Branles de Champagne coupés*. They play a certain other number in succession, which they call *Branles de Camp* and *Branles de Hainault*, and another succession which they call *Branles d'Avignon*. And, according to the number of fresh compositions and novelties of which they make use, so they devise certain suites, giving them such names as they please.

Capriol. Give me the tabulation of all these suites.

Arbeau. I shall not give you any tabulation of them ; you must learn them by heart yourself under the guidance of some excellent musicians, or from your companions. And when you have been taught and wish to dance them at some festival, you will ask the musicians for the suite you wish to dance by its name, and they will play it for you. All the same, I warn you that if you wish to dance these *Branles coupés* well, you must learn the airs by heart, and sing them in your mind to the viol.

Capriol. At least give me the tabulation of two or three, for, by this means, I shall more easily understand the others.

Arbeau. Very well, here is the tabulation of the *Branles de Cassandre* and *de Pinagay*, the first and second of the suite of *Branles de Champagne coupés* which are danced in duple time lightly and without *petits sauts* (like the *Branles de Camp*, *Branles de Hainault* and *Branles d'Avignon*) ; or better, dance them like the *Branles du Haut Barrois*, with *petits sauts*.

Tabulation of the *Branle Coupé* called *Cassandre*

Air of the *Branle Coupé* called *Cassandre*.

Movements suitable for dancing this *Branle*

A	1. *Pied largi gauche.*	These four steps make a *double à gauche.*
	2. *Pied droit approché.*	
	3. *Pied largi gauche.*	
	4. *Pieds joints.*	
	5. *Pied largi droit.*	These four steps make a *double à droite.*
	6. *Pied gauche approché.*	
	7. *Pied largi droit.*	
	8. *Pieds joints.*	
B	1. *Pied largi gauche.*	These four steps make a *double à gauche.*
	2. *Pied droit approché.*	
	3. *Pied largi gauche.*	
	4. *Pieds joints.*	
	5. *Pied largi droit.*	These four steps make a *double à droite.*
	6. *Pied gauche approché.*	
	7. *Pied largi droit.*	
	8. *Pieds joints.*	

C
1. *Pied largi gauche.*
2. *Pieds joints.*
These two steps make a *simple à gauche.*
3. *Pied largi droit.*
4. *Pied gauche approché.*
5. *Pied largi droit.*
6. *Pieds joints.*
These four steps make a *double à droite.*

Tabulation of the *Branle Coupé* called *Pinagay*

Air of the *Branle de Pinagay*

Movements suitable for dancing this *Branle*

A
1. *Pied largi gauche.*
2. *Pied droit approché.*
3. *Pied largi gauche.*
4. *Pieds joints.*
These four steps make a *double à gauche.*
5. *Pied en l'air gauche.*

B
1. *Pied largi gauche.*
2. *Pied droit approché.*
3. *Pied largi gauche.*
4. *Pieds joints.*
These four steps make a *double à gauche.*
5. *Pied en l'air gauche.*
6. *Pied en l'air droit.*
7. *Pied en l'air gauche.*

C
1. *Pied largi gauche.*
2. *Pied droit approché.*
3. *Pied largi gauche.*
4. *Pieds joints.*
These four steps make a *double à gauche.*
5. *Pied largi droit.*
6. *Pied gauche approché.*
7. *Pied largi droit.*
8. *Pieds joints.*
These four steps make a *double à droite.*

Capriol. I believe you know all the movements of the *Branles coupés?*

Arbeau. When I first came to live in the town of Langres, nothing was spoken of but dances, masquerades and gaiety. We had Master Claudin, who played several instruments divinely, and made us practise with a right good will. But for some time, I have encountered nothing but sorrow, which has made me old and grave. In those days we danced, among other *Branles coupés*, the *Branle de la Guerre*, the *Branle d'Aridan*, the *Branle de Charlotte*, and an infinity of others.

Capriol. How did you dance the *Branles* of which you speak ?

Arbeau. You will see by their tabulations.

Tabulation of the *Branle Coupé* called *Charlotte*

Air of the *Branle de Charlotte*

Movements required for dancing this *Branle*

A
1. *Pied largi gauche.*
2. *Pied droit approché.*
3. *Pied largi gauche.*
4. *Pieds joints.*
5. *Pied en l'air gauche.*
6. *Pied en l'air droit.*

(1–4) These four steps make a *double à gauche*.

B
1. *Pied largi droit.*
2. *Pied gauche approché.*
3. *Pied largi droit.*
4. *Pieds joints.*

These four steps make a *double à droite*.

C
1. *Pied largi gauche.*
2. *Pied droit approché.*
3. *Pied largi gauche.*
4. *Pieds joints.*

These four steps make a *double à gauche*.

Continuation of the Air

Continuation of the Movements

C
5. *Pied en l'air gauche.*
6. *Pied en l'air droit.*

D
1. *Pied largi droit.*
2. *Pied gauche approché.* — These two steps make a *simple à droite.*
3. *Pied en l'air gauche.*
4. *Pied en l'air droit.*
5. *Pied en l'air gauche.*

E
1. *Pied largi gauche.*
2. *Pied droit approché.* — These two steps make a *simple à gauche.*
3. *Pied en l'air droit.*
4. *Pied in l'air gauche.*
5. *Pied en l'air droit.*

F
1. *Pied largi droit.*
2. *Pied gauche approché.*
3. *Pied largi droit.*
4. *Pieds joints.* — These four steps make a *double à droite.*

And you will continue by repeating as at the beginning; and note that if you wish to dance it in the manner of the *Branle du Haut Barrois*, you should make *petits sauts* or leave the crotchets empty.

Tabulation of the *Branle Coupé De la Guerre*

Air of the *Branle Coupé De la Guerre*

Movements required for dancing this *Branle*

A
1. *Pied largi gauche.*
2. *Pied droit approché.*
3. *Pied largi gauche.*
4. *Pieds joints.* — These four steps make a *double à gauche.*
5. *Pied largi droit.*
6. *Pied gauche approché.*
7. *Pied largi droit.*
8. *Pieds joints.* — These four steps make a *double à droite.*

B
1. *Pied largi gauche.*
2. *Pied droit approché.*
3. *Pied largi gauche.*
4. *Pieds joints.* — These four steps make a *double à gauche.*
5. *Pied largi droit.*
6. *Pied gauche approché.*
7. *Pied largi droit.*
8. *Pieds joints.* — These four steps make a *double à droite.*

Continuation of the Air

Continuation of the Movements

C

1. *Pied largi gauche.*
2. *Pied droit approché.*
3. *Pied largi gauche.*
4. *Pieds joints.*

These four steps make a *double à gauche.*

5. *Pied largi droit.*
6. *Pied gauche approché.*
7. *Pied largi droit.*
8. *Pieds joints.*

These four steps make a *double à droite.*

D

1. *Pied largi gauche.*
2. *Pieds joints.*
3. *Pied largi droit.*
4. *Pieds joints.*
5. *Pied largi gauche.*
6. *Pied droit approché.*
7. *Pied largi gauche.*
8. *Pieds joints.*

(5–8) These four steps make a *double à gauche.*

E

1. *Pied largi droit.*
2. *Pieds joints.*
3. *Pied largi gauche.*
4. *Pieds joints.*
5. *Pied largi droit.*
6. *Pied gauche approché.*
7. *Pied largi droit.*
8. *Pieds joints.*

(5–8) These four steps make a *double à droite.*

F

1. *Pied largi gauche.*
2. *Pieds joints.*
3. *Grue gauche.*
4. *Grue droite.*
5. *Grue gauche.*
6. *Pieds joints.*
7. *Saut majeur* with *capriole.*

Tabulation of the *Branle Coupé* called *Aridan*

Air of the *Branle Coupé* called *Aridan*

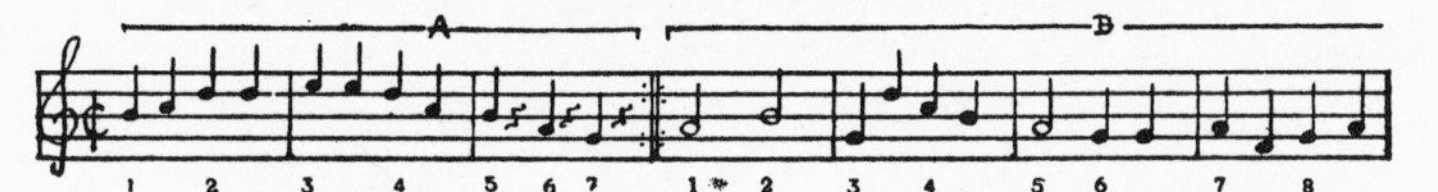

Movements required for dancing this *Branle*

A
1. *Pied largi gauche.*
2. *Pied droit approché.*
3. *Pied largi gauche.*
4. *Pieds joints.*
5. *Pied en l'air gauche.*
6. *Pied en l'air droit.*
7. *Pied en l'air gauche.*

(1–4) These four steps make a *double à gauche.*

B
1. *Pied largi gauche.*
2. *Pied droit approché.*
3. *Pied largi gauche.*
4. *Pieds joints.*
5. *Pied largi droit.*
6. *Pieds joints.*
7. *Pied largi gauche.*
8. *Pieds joints.*

(1–4) These four steps make a *double à gauche.*
(5–6) These two steps make a *simple à droite.*
(7–8) These two steps make a *simple à gauche.*

Continuation of the Air

Continuation of the Movements

B
9. *Pied largi droit.*
10. *Pieds joints.*

(9–10) These two steps make a *simple à droite.*

C
1. *Pied largi gauche.*
2. *Pied droit approché.*
3. *Pied largi gauche.*
4. *Pieds joints.*
5. *Pied en l'air gauche.*
6. *Pied en l'air droit.*

(1–4) These four steps make a *double à gauche.*

D
1. *Pied largi droit.*
2. *Pied gauche approché.*
3. *Pied largi droit.*
4. *Pieds joints.*

These four steps make a *double à droite*.

E
1. *Pied largi gauche.*
2. *Pied droit approché.*
3. *Pied largi gauche.*
4. *Grue droite.*
5. *Pied largi droit.*
6. *Pied gauche approché.*
7. *Grue gauche.*
8. Rest.

Many *Branles* take their name from the country where they are commonly danced. The Poitevins dance their *Branles de Poitou*, the Scots their *Branles d'Ecosse*, the Bretons the *Branles* which they call the *Trihory* or *Passe-pied.*

Capriol. I await the tabulations of them.

BRANLE DE POITOU

Arbeau. Some ignorant people have corrupted the movements of the *Branle de Poitou* so that I cannot follow them, but I will give you the tabulation as I formerly danced them with the young girls of Poitiers. This *Branle* is danced in triple time, always moving to the left without going to the right. I will only give you the beginning of the air, because the rest of it, and all the other *Branles*, of which there are a great number, have the same movements.

Air of the *Branle de Poitou*

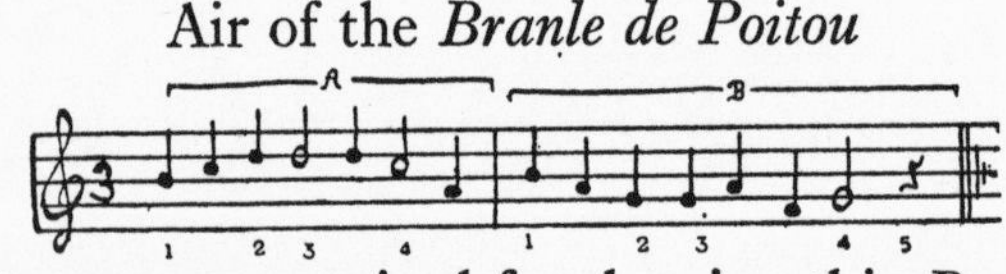

Movements required for dancing this *Branle*

A
1. *Pied en l'air droit.*
2. *Pied en l'air gauche.*
3. *Pied en l'air droit.*
4. *Pied en l'air gauche.*

B
1. *Pied en l'air droit.*
2. *Pied en l'air gauche.*
3. *Pied en l'air droit.*
4. *Pied en l'air gauche.*
5. Rest.

Capriol. Do they no longer make divisions in this *Branle de Poitou?* I have heard it said that the Poitevin girls divide it by making a pleasant noise with their sabots.

Arbeau. In truth, they still stamp in the second and third bars of triple time (which contain six crotchets), to each of which they execute six *pieds en l'air* alternately to right and left, as you see below.

Continuation of the same Air

Divided Movements

A
1. *Pied en l'air droit.*
2. *Pied en l'air gauche.*
3. *Pied en l'air droit.*
4. *Pied en l'air gauche.*
5. *Pied en l'air droit.*

B
1. *Pied en l'air gauche.*
2. *Pied en l'air droit.*
3. *Pied en l'air gauche.*
4. *Pied en l'air droit.*
5. *Pied en l'air gauche.*
6. Rest.

BRANLE D'ECOSSE

The *Branles d'Ecosse* were in fashion about twenty years ago. Musicians have a suite consisting of a number of these *Branles*, differing in their movements, which you can learn from them or from your companions. They are danced in quick duple time, as you see in the tabulations of these two *Branles* following, which are the first and second in the suite.

Tabulation of the *Branle d'Ecosse*

Air of the first *Branle d'Ecosse*

Movements for dancing this first *Branle*

	Steps	
A	1. *Pied largi gauche.* 2. *Pied droit approché.* 3. *Pied largi gauche.* 4. *Pied croisé droit.*	These four steps make a *double à gauche.*
	5. *Pied largi droit.* 6. *Pied gauche approché.* 7. *Pied largi droit.* 8. *Pied croisé gauche.*	These four steps make a *double à droite.*
B	1. *Pied largi gauche.* 2. *Pied croisé droit.*	These two steps make a *simple à gauche.*
	3. *Pied largi droit.* 4. *Pied croisé gauche.*	These two steps make a *simple à droite.*
	5. *Pied largi gauche.* 6. *Pied droit approché.* 7. *Pied largi gauche.* 8. *Pied croisé droit.*	These four steps make a *double à gauche.*
C	1. *Pied largi droit.* 2. *Pied gauche approché.* 3. *Pied largi droit.* 4. *Pied croisé gauche.*	These four steps make a *double à droite.*
	5. *Pied largi gauche.* 6. *Pied croisé droit.*	These two steps make a *simple à gauche.*
	7. *Pied largi droit.* 8. *Pied croisé gauche.*	These two steps make a *simple à droite.*

Air of the second *Branle d'Ecosse*

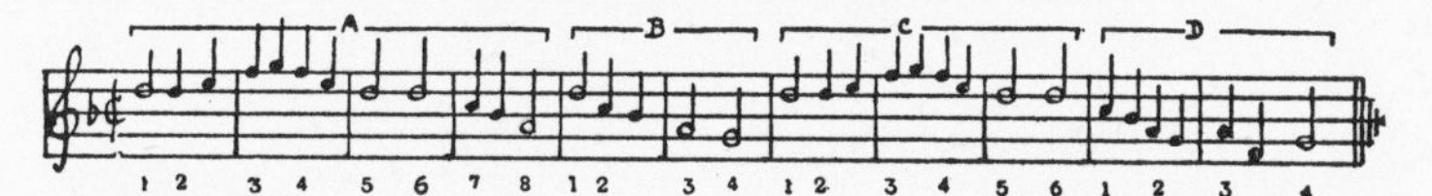

Movements for dancing this second *Branle*

	Movements	
A	1. *Pied largi gauche.* 2. *Pied droit approché.* 3. *Pied largi gauche.* 4. *Pied croisé droit.*	These four steps make a *double à gauche.*
	5. *Pied largi droit.* 6. *Pied croisé gauche.*	These two steps make a *simple à droite.*
	7. *Pied largi gauche.* 8. *Pied croisé droit.*	These two steps make a *simple à gauche.*
B	1. *Pied largi droit.* 2. *Pied gauche approché.* 3. *Pied largi droit.* 4. *Pied croisé gauche.*	These four steps make a *double à droite.*
C	1. *Pied largi gauche.* 2. *Pied droit approché.* 3. *Pied largi gauche.* 4. *Pied croisé droit.*	These four steps make a *double à gauche.*
	5. *Pied largi droit.* 6. *Pied gauche croisé.*	These two steps make a *simple à droite.*
D	1. *Pied en l'air droit.* 2. *Pied en l'air gauche.* 3. *Pied en l'air droit.* 4. *Saut majeur* and *capriole.*	

TRIHORY DE BRETAGNE

This *Branle* is little or never practised nowadays. If some day you should happen to dance it, it will be in light duple time, as this tabulation shows you. I learned to dance it a long while ago from a young Breton who lived with me when a student at Poitiers.

Capriol. I am very pleased to learn this *Trihory.* One cannot do better than to have knowledge of a great many things.

Tabulation of the *Branle* called *Trihory*

Air of this *Branle*

Movements for dancing this *Branle* called *Trihory*

1. *Pied largi gauche.*
2. *Pied droit approché.*
3. *Pied largi gauche.*
4. *Pied en l'air gauche.*

These four steps make a *double à gauche.*

5. Spring to the left and fall in the position *pieds joints.*
6. *Pied en l'air gauche.*
7. *Pied en l'air droit.*
8. *Pied en l'air gauche.*

And thus you will continue by repeating the movements as before.

In place of the three *pieds en l'air*, which are made at the end of this *Trihory*, you will hold yourself firm on tip-toe, and, bringing your heels together in place of *marque pied gauche*, turn them to the right. In place of *marque pied droite*, turn your heels to the left; and in place of the last *pied en l'air gauche*, turn them to the right, at the same time raising your left foot in the air. And, that you may see it clearly at a glance, I will give you the tabulation for the three last notes of the air.

1. Turn both heels to the right.
2. Turn both heels to the left.
3. Turn both heels to the right, at the same time execute a *pied en l'air gauche.*

There are still many kinds of *Branles* of which I am minded to give you the tabulations, since you are eager to learn a great many of them. And you must know that when some new *Branle* is done, which they call a ballet, to be used in a masquerade or some festival, the young men immediately show it to their companions and give it a name of their own.

To this number belong the tabulations of the *Branles* which follow, which *Branles* and ballets are for the most part danced with certain expressions, mimings and gestures, and on this account may be termed mimed *Branles*. We will begin with the *Branle de Malte*.

BRANLE DE MALTE

Some Knights of Malta devised a ballet for a court masquerade where there were an equal number of ladies and gentlemen, dressed in the Turkish fashion, who danced a *Branle* in a Round with certain gestures and twistings of the body, which they called *Branle de Malte*. It is about forty years ago since this dance was first performed in France. The air and movements are in slow duple time, as you see in this tabulation.

Capriol. Perhaps the inhabitants of Malta customarily practise this dance, so that it is not a ballet devised for a special occasion.

Arbeau. I cannot believe that it is other than a ballet, because it is danced with certain gestures, mimings and expressions of the features which have persisted during all the time it has been in use. However that may be, the following tabulation will aid you.

Tabulation of the *Branle de Malte*

Air of the *Branle de Malte*

Movements for dancing this *Branle*

A
1. *Pied largi gauche.*
2. *Pied droit approché.*
3. *Pied largi gauche.*
4. *Pieds joints.*

These four steps make a *double à gauche*.

5. *Pied largi droit.*
6. *Pieds joints.*

These two steps make a *simple à droite*.

B	1. *Pied gauche avancé.* 2. *Pied droit avancé.* 3. *Pied gauche avancé.* 4. *Pied droit avancé.* 5. *Pied gauche avancé,* with a *grue droite.*	During these movements the dancers gesticulate, coming together in close formation in the middle of the room as if they wish to have a confabulation.
C	1. *Pied droit avancé.* 2. *Grue gauche.* 3. *Pied gauche avancé.* 4. *Grue droite.*	Here they leave go of each other's hands and turn to the left.
	5. *Pied en l'air gauche.* 6. *Pied en l'air droit.* 7. *Pied en l'air gauche.* 8. *Pieds joints.*	After the dancers have made this turn, they fall into the position *pieds joints* and join hands again, repeating the dance from the beginning.

You must notice that every time this *Branle* is repeated new expressions and gestures must be made, such as touchings of the hands on one occasion, and, on another, raisings of them in the air in pretended admiration, with the head uplifted; and so on, as it pleases the dancers to devise.

BRANLE DES LAVANDIÈRES

This mimed *Branle*, called the *Branle des Lavandières*, is danced in duple time, and is called so because the dancers, clapping their hands, make a noise like that produced by the bats of the washer-women on the banks of the Seine in Paris.[1]

Capriol. Are there many kinds of mimings in this *Branle des Lavandières* of which you speak?

Arbeau. You will see by the tabulation the different kinds that are done. But there is no change in these when the *Branle* is repeated, as at the beginning, of which I should have warned you as soon as you asked for the tabulation.

[1] Compare the *Carillon de Dunkerque*, in which the dancers stamp their feet and clap their hands to simulate the sound of bells. A description of this dance will be found in G. Desrat, *Dictionnaire de la Danse*, 1895 (p. 74), and E. Giraudet, *La Danse, etc.*, N.D. (p. 163).

Tabulation of the *Branle des Lavandières*

Air of this *Branle*

Movements for dancing this *Branle*

A

1. *Pied largi gauche.*
2. *Pied droit approché.*
3. *Pied largi gauche.*
4. *Pieds joints.*

These four steps make a *double à gauche.*

5. *Pied largi droit.*
6. *Pied gauche approché.*
7. *Pied largi droit.*
8. *Pieds joints.*

These four steps make a *double à droite.*

B

1. *Pied largi gauche.*
2. *Pieds joints.*
3. *Pied largi droit.*
4. *Pieds joints.*

During these two *simples* the women hold their sides and the men shake their fingers at them, and, on the repetition of the *simples*, the men hold their sides and the women shake their fingers at them.

C

1. *Pied largi gauche.*
2. *Pied droit approché.*

During these two steps all the dancers clap their hands.

Continuation of the Air

Continuation of the Movements

C

3. *Pied largi gauche.*
4. *Pieds joints.*

During these two steps all the dancers clap their hands.

5. *Pied largi droit.*
6. *Pied gauche approché.*
7. *Pied largi droit.*
8. *Pieds joints.*

These four steps make a *double à droite.*

D

1. *Pied largi gauche.*
2. *Pied droit approché.*
3. *Pied largi gauche.*
4. *Pieds joints.*

During these four steps all the dancers again clap their hands.

5. *Pied en l'air gauche.*
6. *Pied en l'air droit.*
7. *Pied en l'air gauche.*
8. *Saut majeur*, coming to the ground in the position *pieds joints.*

During these four steps the dancers leave go of each other's hands, each turning to the left; and after the *saut* they join hands again and recommence the dance from the beginning.

BRANLE DES POIS

Among the *Branles* with mimings and gestures there is the *Branles des Pois*, otherwise called the *Branle de Margueritotte*, which is danced in a light duple time like the *Branle Commun*, or like the *Branle du Haut Barrois*, as you wish. It requires an equal number of men and women, who dance according to the following tabulation, in which I have placed for you notes of suitable gestures and mimings which are not difficult.

Tabulation of the *Branle des Pois*

Air of this *Branle*

Movements for dancing this *Branle*

A

1. *Pied largi gauche.*
2. *Pied droit approché.*
3. *Pied largi gauche.*
4. *Pieds joints.*

These four steps make a *double à gauche.*

5. *Pied largi droit.*
6. *Pied gauche approché.*
7. *Pied largi droit.*
8. *Pieds joints.*

These four steps make a *double à droite.*

	Steps	
B	1. *Saut majeur* by the men.	During these two steps the women do not move.
	2. *Pieds joints.*	
	3. *Saut majeur* by the women.	During these two steps the men do not move.
	4. *Pieds joints.*	
	5. *Pied largi gauche.*	While the men execute these three *sauts* the women do not move.
	6. *Petit saut.*	
	7. *Pieds joints.*	
	8. *Petit saut.*	
	9. *Pieds joints.*	
	10. *Petit saut.*	
	11. *Pieds joints.*	
C	1. *Saut majeur* by the women.	During these two steps the men do not move.
	2. *Pieds joints.*	
	3. *Saut majeur* by the men.	During these two steps the women do not move.
	4. *Pieds joints.*	
	5. *Pied largi gauche.*	While the women make these three *sauts* the men make no movement.
	6. *Petit saut.*	
	7. *Pieds joints.*	
	8. *Petit saut.*	
	9. *Pieds joints.*	
	10. *Petit saut.*	
	11. *Pieds joints.*	

BRANLE DES HERMITES

I shall place among the mimed *Branles* the *Branle des Hermites*, which is called so because gestures are made in it similar to those which hermits make when they greet someone. I believe that it is derived from some masquerade of former days, in which were young men dressed like hermits. I advise you not to disguise yourself in such garments, nor to counterfeit the faces of monks, because their clothes and persons should be respected. On this occasion I will pass it over.

Capriol. I will gladly follow your advice. But do not withhold from me the tabulation of it as it was danced.

Arbeau. I am very willing to satisfy your desire, because your only object in learning the dance is that you may not be ignorant of it. This *Branle* was danced in a moderate duple time in the form which you see below.

Tabulation of the *Branle des Hermites*

Air of the *Branle des Hermites*

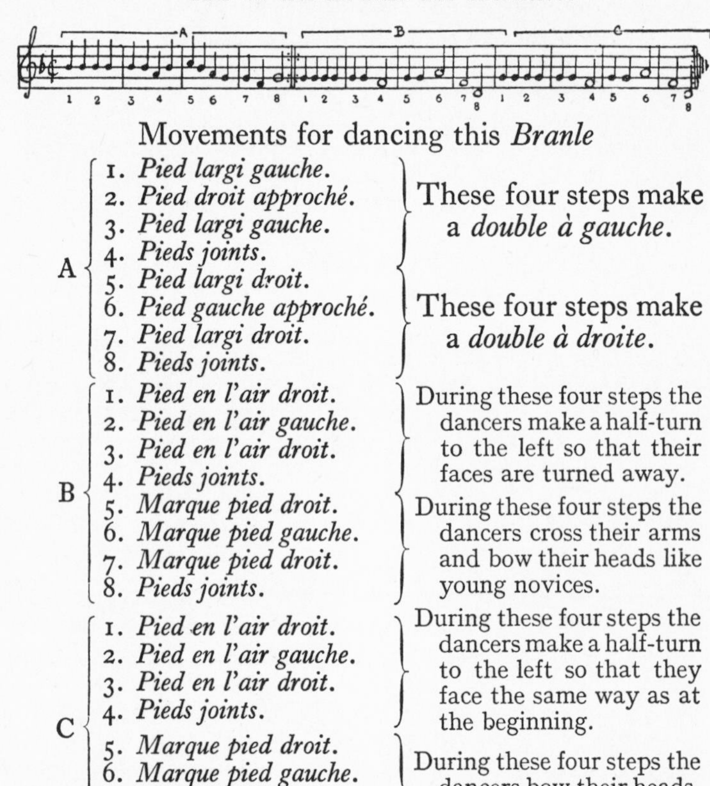

Movements for dancing this *Branle*

	Steps	
A	1. *Pied largi gauche.*	These four steps make a *double à gauche.*
	2. *Pied droit approché.*	
	3. *Pied largi gauche.*	
	4. *Pieds joints.*	
	5. *Pied largi droit.*	These four steps make a *double à droite.*
	6. *Pied gauche approché.*	
	7. *Pied largi droit.*	
	8. *Pieds joints.*	
B	1. *Pied en l'air droit.*	During these four steps the dancers make a half-turn to the left so that their faces are turned away.
	2. *Pied en l'air gauche.*	
	3. *Pied en l'air droit.*	
	4. *Pieds joints.*	
	5. *Marque pied droit.*	During these four steps the dancers cross their arms and bow their heads like young novices.
	6. *Marque pied gauche.*	
	7. *Marque pied droit.*	
	8. *Pieds joints.*	
C	1. *Pied en l'air droit.*	During these four steps the dancers make a half-turn to the left so that they face the same way as at the beginning.
	2. *Pied en l'air gauche.*	
	3. *Pied en l'air droit.*	
	4. *Pieds joints.*	
	5. *Marque pied droit.*	During these four steps the dancers bow their heads, as we have said above.
	6. *Marque pied gauche.*	
	7. *Marque pied droit.*	
	8. *Pieds joints.*	

BRANLE DE CHANDELIER

This *Branle*, otherwise termed *Branle de la Torche*,[1] is danced in moderate duple time with the same steps as those of the *Allemande*. Whoever wishes to dance it takes a candlestick with a lighted candle, or a torch or brand, and dances or walks forward once or twice round the room, looking here

[1] This *branle* is mentioned by Brantôme in his *Vie des Dames Galantes.* See *Discours Septiesme :* "le soir au bal il la voulut mener danser le bransle de la torche, & puis la fit mener danser à un autre la gaillarde, &

and there for the damsel he wishes to dance with him. When he has chosen one who pleases him, they dance together for a little while, and at last he disposes of her by leaving her at the end of the room and, making her a *révérence*, gives into her hands the candlestick, torch or brand, and retires dancing to his place.

The damsel, holding the candlestick, does as she has seen the young man do, and dances away to choose another man, who eventually takes her place, receiving the candlestick from her; and in this way all invite each other in turn to dance.

Tabulation of the *Branle de la Torche*

Air of the *Branle de la Torche*

Movements for dancing this *Branle*

A
1. *Pied gauche avancé.*
2. *Pied droit avancé.*
3. *Pied gauche avancé.*
4. *Grue droite.*
5. *Pied droit avancé.*
6. *Pied gauche avancé.*
7. *Pied droit avancé.*
8. *Grue gauche.*

B
1. *Pied gauche avancé.*
2. *Pied droit avancé.*
3. *Pied gauche avancé.*
4. *Grue droite.*
5. *Pied droit avancé.*
6. *Pied gauche avancé.*
7. *Pied droit avancé.*
8. *Grue gauche.*

During these steps and movements the dancer makes one or two circles round the room, seeking whom he will choose to give the candle to.

les autres bransles, là où elle monstra sa disposition & dexterité mieux que jamais avec sa taille, qui estoit tres-belle . . ."

The *Branle de la Torche*, or Torch Dance, was frequently danced at the Court of Philip the Good, Duke of Burgundy. A painting of this dance by a Flemish master of the XVth century is reproduced in Paul Lacroix, *Les mœurs et usages au Moyen-Age et à l'époque de la Renaissance*, and in Lilly Grove, *Dancing*, 1895, p. 251. There is another representation of this dance, attributed to Simon Bening, in a Flemish Book of Hours (the "Golf Book"), preserved in the British Museum. It is reproduced in colour in C. J. Sharp and A. P. Oppé, *The Dance*, 1924. *Vide:* plate facing p. 14.

C
1. *Pied gauche avancé.*
2. *Grue droite.*
3. *Pied droit avancé.*
4. *Grue gauche.*

During these four steps the dancer looks here and there, seeking the partner he prefers.

Capriol. This dance is one which permits all in the company to dance as you said of the *Gaillarde* called *Lyonaise.*

BRANLE DES SABOTS

Rosinus, in his work on Roman Antiquities, relates that according to Book VII. of Dionysius of Halicarnassus, dancers, during the pomps and splendours of the Public Games at Rome, walked in a procession bearing *tibiæ*, harps and barbytons.[1] One of them walked in front of the others and showed them a certain order of dances and mimings, which all the others copied, endeavouring to imitate the leader as if they were playing at puppets. A masquerade after this manner was given at this town of Langres, in which a female buffoon-in-chief preceded three clowns and prescribed them certain gestures, then turned round to ascertain if the three clowns, her children, did them exactly as she did. They danced the *Branle des Sabots*, which they had adapted to it.

Capriol. How is this *Branle des Sabots* danced ?

Arbeau. In duple time, like the *Branle Double*, by making four steps to the left, then four to the right. Then two *simples* and three taps of the feet, which are repeated.

Tabulation of the *Branle des Sabots*

Air of the *Branle des Sabots*

Movements of this *Branle*

A
1. *Pied largi gauche.*
2. *Pied droit approché.*
3. *Pied largi gauche.*
4. *Pieds joints.*

These four steps make a *double à gauche.*

[1] A kind of lyre.

A:
5. *Pied largi droit.*
6. *Pied gauche approché.*
7. *Pied largi droit.*
8. *Pieds joints.*

These four steps make a *double à droite.*

B:
1. *Pied largi gauche.*
2. *Pieds joints.*

These two steps make a *simple à gauche.*

3. *Pied largi droit.*
4. *Pieds joints.*

These two steps make a *simple à droite.*

5. Tap the right foot.
6. Tap the right foot.
7. Tap the right foot.

In place of these tappings of the feet, other mimings can be made as desired.

In this *Branle des Sabots* the men make, if they wish, the first three taps of the feet, and during this the women do nothing ; on the repeat the women make the other three taps of the feet, and the men do not move. Then all together recommence the *Branle* with new mimings according to their fancy.

Capriol. These taps of the feet remind me of horses when they wish to disturb the water, or of palfreys when they are kept waiting for their peck of oats.

BRANLE DES CHEVAUX

Arbeau. In this connection I have seen them dance a *Branle* called *Branle des Chevaux*, in which taps of the feet are made as in the preceding *Branle*, and it seems to me that the air is similar to the one which you see in the following tabulation, which is danced in duple time, like the *Branle Commun*, the young man holding the damsel by both hands. The beginning of the air of the *Branle* was as you see noted here, and was danced by four *doubles à gauche* and four *doubles à droite*.

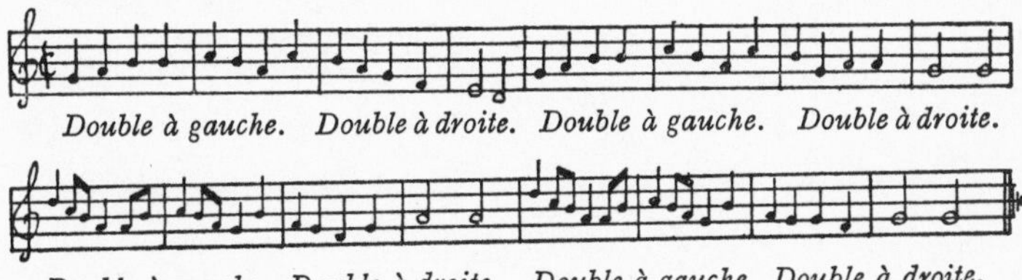

Tabulation of the rest of this *Branle*

Continuation of the Air

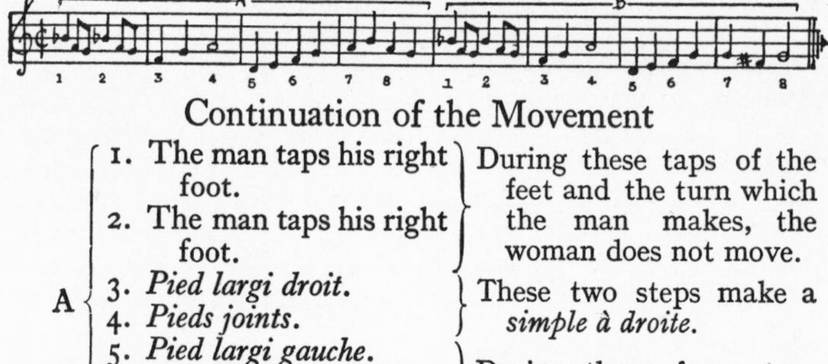

Continuation of the Movement

	Steps	
A	1. The man taps his right foot. 2. The man taps his right foot.	During these taps of the feet and the turn which the man makes, the woman does not move.
	3. *Pied largi droit.* 4. *Pieds joints.*	These two steps make a *simple à droite.*
	5. *Pied largi gauche.* 6. *Pied droit approché.* 7. *Pied largi gauche.* 8. *Pieds joints.*	During these four steps the man makes a turn to the left.
B	1. The woman taps her right foot. 2. The woman taps her right foot.	During these taps of the feet and the turn which the woman makes, the man does not move.
	3. *Pied largi droit.* 4. *Pieds joints.*	These two steps make a *simple à droite.*
	5. *Pied largi gauche.* 6. *Pied droit approché.* 7. *Pied largi gauche.* 8. *Pieds joints.*	During these four steps the woman makes a turn to the left.

This done, the dancers join hands again, and repeat from the beginning.

BRANLE DE LA MONTARDE

Formerly we danced a mimed *Branle* called *Branle de la Montarde*, which we danced in duple time with *petits sauts*, as in the *Branle du Haut Barrois*, going always to the left without moving to the right. The dancers consist of an equal number of men and women. One of the men leads in front, one of the women brings up the rear, and they all dance together four *doubles à gauche*. The one who leads makes a turn, separating himself from the others ; then the second makes a turn and joins the first. Then the third makes his turn, joining the second, and so on. In this way every one taking part in the dance makes his or her turn. And when the last has made her turn, the first makes a Hay[1] by passing in front of the women and behind the men, and places himself at the rear, taking the last woman by the hand. And while he makes this Hay, all the others, in front of and behind whom he has passed, join hands and repeat the *Branle* as at the beginning. By doing so, the woman who was the second now finds herself the first, and she must do the same as the original leader at the beginning ; thus each one becomes the first and last in turn. And when the last has come to the front and made her Hay, she again finds herself last, as she was at the beginning. Then the musicians conclude the *Branle* of which the tabulation is given here.

Tabulation of the *Branle de la Montarde*

Air of the *Branle de la Montarde*

Movements for dancing this *Branle*

A
1. *Pied largi gauche.*
2. *Petit saut.*
3. *Pied droit approché.*
4. *Petit saut.*

These four steps make a *double à gauche.*

5. *Pied largi gauche.*
6. *Petit saut.*
7. *Pied joints.*
8. *Petit saut.*

B
1. *Pied largi gauche.*
2. *Petit saut.*
3. *Pied droit approché.*
4. *Petit saut.*

These four steps make a *double à gauche.*

[1] The late Cecil Sharp defines the Hay as "the rhythmical interlacing in serpentine fashion of two groups of dancers, moving in single file and in opposite directions." (*Vide :* C. J. Sharp, *The Country Dance Book*, Part VI., N.D., p. 28, *et seq.*, for a description, illustrated with many diagrams, of the different forms of this figure.)

Hogarth explains the Hay as "a cypher of S's, or a number of serpentine lines interlacing, or intervolving each other." (*Vide :* William Hogarth, *The Analysis of Beauty*, 1753, p. 150.) *An Analysis of Country Dancing* (1811), by Thomas Wilson, also contains many diagrams of the Hay (*vide :* pp. 60–65).

	Steps	
B	5. *Pied largi gauche.*	
	6. *Petit saut.*	
	7. *Pieds joints.*	
	8. *Petit saut.*	
C	1. *Pied largi gauche.*	These four steps make a *double à gauche.*
	2. *Petit saut.*	
	3. *Pied droit approché.*	
	4. *Petit saut.*	
	5. *Pied largi gauche.*	
	6. *Petit saut.*	
	7. *Pieds joints.*	
	8. *Petit saut.*	
D	1. *Pied largi gauche.*	These four steps make a *double à gauche.*
	2. *Petit saut.*	
	3. *Pied droit approché.*	
	4. *Petit saut.*	
	5. *Pied largi gauche.*	
	6. *Petit saut.*	
	7. *Pieds joints.*	
	8. Rest.	
E	1. *Pied en l'air gauche.*	The instrumentalists repeat this close as many times as there are dancers, so that each can make his turn. When they begin the *Branle* again the leader makes the Hay and the others join hands again to dance.
	2. *Pied en l'air droit.*	
	3. *Pied en l'air gauche.*	
	4. *Pieds joints.*	

Capriol. This *Branle de la Montarde*, then, is the one which damsels call *La Haye?*

BRANLE DE LA HAYE

Arbeau. The dance, *Branle de la Haye*, of which you speak, is another one. It is danced in duple time, like the *Courante*. The dancers, singly and in succession, first dance the air in the manner of the *Courante*, and at the end, interlace and make the Hay. I will give you in the first place the air of the *Courante*, which, as you know, consists of two *simples* and a *double*. Then I will give you the air which the musicians play at the conclusion, during which the dancers interlace.

Tabulation of the dance called *La Haye*

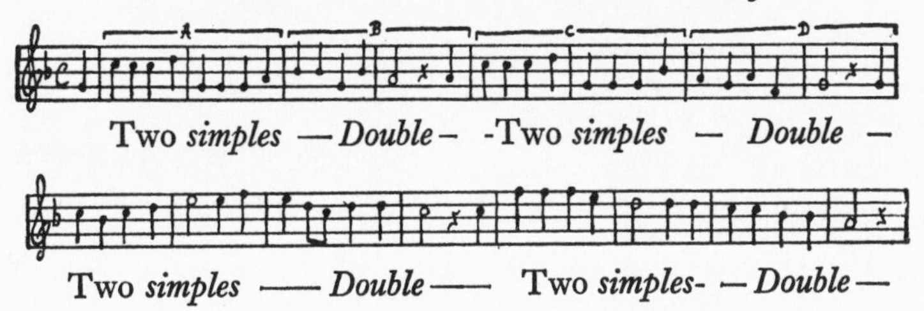

Air and Movements of the Hay

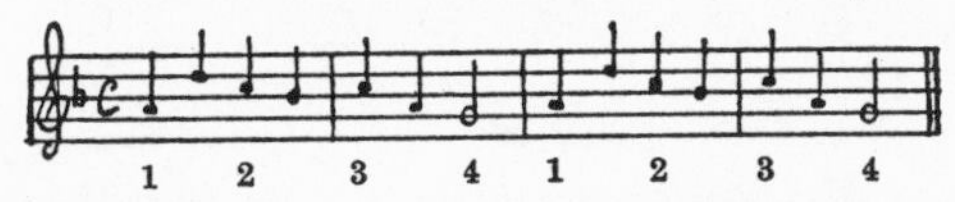

1. *Pied gauche avancé.*
2. *Pied droit avancé.*
3. *Pied gauche avancé.*
4. *Pieds joints.*

During these four steps, and those that follow in like manner, the dancers make the Hay, changing places with one another.

1. *Pied droit avancé.*
2. *Pied gauche avancé.*
3. *Pied droit avancé.*
4. *Pieds joints.*

During these four steps the leader of the dance continues the Hay until he comes to the last person, and the musicians continue to play till the Hay is concluded.

Capriol. I cannot understand what you tell me of this Hay.

Arbeau. You will easily understand it thus. Let us suppose there are three dancers (it is the least number there can be), and imagine that they are represented by the letters A, B, and C.

A B C

In the first four steps of the air of *the Hay*, A and B change places, passing to their left ; then in the second four steps, A and C change places, passing to their right, so that they will be found placed thus as you see here.

B C A

This done, B and C change places as before ; then B and

A, so that in the third four bars of *the Hay* they will be found disposed thus :

C A B

In the four steps following, C will change with A, then C with B, and thus they will be found situated as at the beginning :

A B C

Capriol. If it should happen that the dancers were more than three, would the changing of places be the same as you have just explained ?

Arbeau. You may conclude so. But you must pay attention to what I am going to say to you. Supposing the dancers be seven in number, A, B, C, D, E, F, G ; A, the first, changes with B, the second, and A again changes with C, the third ; and C changes with D, the fourth, so that B is now first. A must then begin to Hay, and changes places with C, who is now the second, and so on.

Capriol. According to what you say, I imagine that C will be the first, and that he must begin his Hay by changing with D, who is now second, at the same time as B changes and makes the Hay with E, the fourth, and so on.

Arbeau. You understand it perfectly. The *Branle de l'Official* will not be so difficult for you.

BRANLE DE L'OFFICIAL

This *Branle*, which has not long been in fashion, is danced in duple time with *petits sauts* like the *Branle du Haut Barrois*, and is begun by a *double à gauche* and a *double à droite* repeated. Then the dancers continue to the left for six *simples*, at the end of which the musicians make the cadence, when the men take the women by the small of the back and make them spring and leap into the air, coming to the ground at the said cadence, the men meanwhile standing firm on their feet to support them. And at such moments, those whose partners will not spring of their own accord, are greatly inconvenienced by the necessity of lifting them.

Tabulation of the *Branle de l'Official*

Air of the *Branle de l'Official*

Movements for dancing this *Branle*

A

1. *Pied largi gauche.*
2. *Petit saut.*
3. *Pied droit approché.*
4. *Petit saut.*
5. *Pied largi gauche.*
6. *Petit saut.*
7. *Pieds joints.*
8. *Petit saut.*

These four steps make a *double à gauche*.

B

1. *Pied largi droit.*
2. *Petit saut.*
3. *Pied gauche approché.*
4. *Petit saut.*
5. *Pied largi droit.*
6. *Petit saut.*
7. *Pieds joints.*
8. *Petit saut.*

These four steps make a *double à droite*.

A

1. *Pied largi gauche.*
2. *Petit saut.*
3. *Pieds joints.*
4. *Petit saut.*
5. *Pied largi gauche.*
6. *Petit saut.*
7. *Pieds joints.*
8. *Petit saut.*

B

1. *Pied largi gauche.*
2. *Petit saut.*
3. *Pieds joints.*
4. *Petit saut.*
5. *Pied largi gauche.*
6. *Petit saut.*
7. *Pieds joints.*
8. *Petit saut.*

During these steps the dancers continue to the left, without going to the right.

C
1. *Pied largi gauche.*
2. *Petit saut.*
3. *Pieds joints.*
4. *Petit saut.*
5. *Pied largi gauche.*
6. *Petit saut.*
7. *Pieds joints.*

During these steps the dancers continue to the left, without going to the right.

D
1. *Pied en l'air gauche.*
2. *Pied en l'air droit.*
3. *Pieds joints.*
4. Pause.

During these four steps the man takes his partner by the small of the back to make her leap into the air, and to accomplish this he turns to the right.

Capriol. I quite understand that this *Branle* is continued by repeating the beginning. But I find it very tiresome that to dance it properly one is dependent in part on the dexterity and agility of the damsel whom one has to help in her jump; and some would dance it who had not sufficient strength.

Arbeau. You will find no great trouble in the *Branles de Gavottes*, in which the damsels need not be raised in the air, but only kissed.

Capriol. That is something which I would do easily and very willingly; and for that reason I wish to learn and know them.

GAVOTTES

Arbeau. A *Gavotte* is a collection of several *Branles Doubles* which musicians have chosen and arranged in a sequence, which you may learn from them or from your companions. To this sequence they have given this name of *Gavottes*. They are danced in duple time with *petits sauts* in the manner of the *Branle du Haut Barrois*, and consist of a *double à droite* and a *double à gauche* like the *Branle Commun*. But the dancers divide the *doubles*, both *à droite* and *à gauche*, by passages taken at will from the *Gaillardes*. When the dancers have danced a little, one of them, with his damsel, goes a little way apart and makes several passages in the middle of the dance in the sight of all the others; then he comes to kiss all the other damsels, and all the young men kiss his damsel, and they return to their proper order. This done, the second dancer does the same; and, in succession, all the others do so.

Some accord the privilege of kissing to the leader of the dance alone, and to the damsel who is his companion. And at the end, the damsel having a chaplet or posy, presents it to one of the dancers, who has to pay the musicians and be the leader of the dance at the next meeting, at which he will have the same privilege ; and so on in turn. I will give you the air of the first *Branle*, and some divisions which you can alter at will.

Tabulation of a *Gavotte*

Air of the *Gavotte*

Movements for dancing the *Gavotte*

A
1. *Pied largi gauche.*
2. *Petit saut.*
3. *Pied droit approché.*
4. *Petit saut.*
5. *Marque pied droit croisé.*
6. *Petit saut.*
7. *Grue droite croisée.*
8. *Petit saut.*

Passage of four steps equivalent to a *double à gauche.*

B
1. *Pieds joints.*
2. *Petit saut.*
3. *Marque pied gauche croisé.*
4. *Marque pied droit croisé.*
5. *Grue droite croisée.*
6. *Petit saut.*
7. *Pieds joints* with *capriole.*

Passage of five steps in the time of four, equivalent to a *double à droite.*

Here is the rest of the air of the first *Branle* of the suite of *Gavottes* as our musicians of Langres play it. You will adapt to it the divisions above or such others as it will please you to select or devise or imitate from good and agile dancers. If this type of dance had been in fashion when my legs were young I should not have failed to make notes about it.

–*Double à gauche*– –*Double à droite.*–

MORISQUES

In my young days, at supper-time in good society, I have seen a daubed and blackened little boy, his forehead bound with a white or yellow scarf, who, with bells on his legs, danced the *Morisques* and, walking the length of the room, made a kind of passage. Then, retracing his steps, he returned to the place where he began and made another new passage, and continued thus, making various passages very agreeable to the onlookers. Macrobius, in his fourteenth chapter of the third book of the *Saturnalia*, declares through Horus that children of noble birth and young girls of the best Roman families danced with the *Crotalum*,[1] which the commentator Badius interprets as little bells, but this translation does not please me, and I rather believe that the *Crotalum* was a little Basque tabor adorned with little bells such as was carried by the Mother of the Gods, or, better, that they were what we call cymbals and a triangle furnished with rings which, when played, made an agreeable noise to accompany the *vieille*. Nevertheless, the ability to perform this dance well was held in high esteem.

Capriol. This verse of Virgil will serve to support your opinion:

[2]Crispum sub Crotalo docta movere latus.

If the poet had meant bells, he would have written *cum* [3] and not *sub*.[4] I beg you to give me a little note of the *Morisques*, and I will teach my lackey to dance them.

Arbeau. Morisques are danced in duple time. Originally they were danced with tappings of the feet, but because the dancers found them too painful they employed tappings of the heels only, holding the toes firm. Some wished to dance them with *marque pieds* and *marque talons* mixed together. In the practice of all three kinds, especially that which depends on tappings of the feet, experience has shown that sooner or later you acquire the gout and similar illnesses; for which reason, this dance has fallen into disuse. I will

[1] The *Crotalum* was a kind of castanet, rattle or clapper used by dancers. In its simplest form it was doubtless a couple of shells pierced with holes and strung together. Brass, wood and split cane were also used as materials. In all probability the *crotalum* differed little from the castanets of to-day.

[2] Skilled in moving her quivering flank beneath the *Crotalum*.

[3] Literally *with*.

[4] Literally *under*.

only give you the air with the movements in a passage ; and as for the other passages, you can learn them from those who are versed in them, but of such persons very few can now be found.

Tabulation of the *Morisques*

Air of the *Morisques*

Movements for dancing the *Morisque*[1]

A
1. Tap the right heel.
2. Tap the left heel.
3. Tap the right heel.
4. Tap the left heel.
5. Tap both heels.[2]
6. Rest.

B
1. Tap the right heel.
2. Tap the left heel.
3. Tap the right heel.
4. Tap the left heel.
5. Tap both heels.
6. Rest.

C
1. Tap the right heel.
2. Tap the left heel.
3. Tap the right heel.
4. Tap the left heel.
5. Tap the right heel.
6. Tap the left heel.
7. Tap the right heel.
8. Tap the left heel.

D
1. Tap the right heel.
2. Tap the left heel.
3. Tap the right heel.
4. Tap the left heel.
5. Tap both heels.
6. Rest.

The dancer keeps his toes firmly together while he taps his heels to make his bells sound, and the tapping of both heels is done without turning to right or left, in the manner of a *pieds joints*.

[1] The late Mr. Cecil Sharp has pointed out that the step used in the *Morisque* is not the normal Morris step, but a curious heel-and-toe movement which, strangely enough, he once noted from a Morris dancer in a Northamptonshire village. *Vide:* C. J. Sharp and A. P. Oppé, *The Dance*, 1924, p. 18.

[2] That is, both heels strike the ground together.

Capriol. As I understand the movements of the *Morisques*, it seems that the dancer does not move from one place.

Arbeau. He must always go forward to the end of the room. And to do this you will note that, after the heel-tapping, which corresponds to a *pieds joints* and cadence, and before the right heel-tapping, the dancer lightly advances his two feet and at the same time executes the right heel-tapping. For, if you consider the matter, the tap of the right heel follows after the *pieds joints*. Note also, that this *Morisque* air is divided into quavers, and on each of them the heels are tapped as shown below.

Capriol. M. Arbeau, I have noticed that, in all the dances of which you have given me the movements, you have never spoken of the *ru de vache*, notwithstanding that you have included it already among the other movements.

Arbeau. That is true, and the reason is because dancers hardly ever use it except sometimes in the dance called *Canaries*, which I should like to describe to you.

CANARIES

Some say that this dance comes from the Canary Isles, and that it is regularly practised there. Others, whose opinion I should prefer to share, hold that it is derived from a ballet composed for a masquerade in which the dancers were dressed as kings and queens of Mauretania, or rather, like savages with plumes dyed in various colours. This is the manner of dancing the *Canaries*. A young man takes a damsel and dancing with her to the phrases of a suitable air, conducts her to the end of the room. This done, he returns to the place where he began, gazing at the damsel the while. He then goes towards her again, making certain passages, and, this done, he returns as before. Then the damsel comes and does the same in front of him, and afterwards returns to the place where she was ; and both continue these goings and comings as many times as the diversity of passages affords them the means. And note that these passages are lively, yet strange and fantastic, resembling in large measure the dances of savages. You will learn them from those who know them, and you can invent new ones for yourself. I shall only give you the air of this dance, and some movements of the passages which the dancers are accustomed to make and which the onlookers take pleasure in seeing.

Tabulation of the dance called *Canaries*

Air of the dance called *Canaries*

Movements for dancing the *Canaries*

A
1. Tap the left foot, making a *pied en l'air droit.*
2. *Marque talon droit.*
3. *Marque pied droit.*
4. Tap the right foot, making a *pied en l'air gauche.*
5. *Marque talon gauche.*
6. *Marque pied gauche.*

B
1. Tap the left foot, making a *pied en l'air droit.*
2. *Marque talon droit.*
3. *Marque pied droit.*
4. Tap the right foot, making a *pied en l'air gauche.*
5. *Marque talon gauche.*
6. *Marque pied gauche.*

The rest of this air is danced in the same manner as above for as long as the dancer continues the movements in front of his partner, going forward and retiring, and concluding in his original position. And observe that, for a second passage, instead of the tappings of the toe one can make a very high *grue*, ending with a dragging of the foot backwards along the ground as if one wished to tread out spittle or to crush a spider.

Capriol. You promised before to give me the *Pavane d'Espagne* after the *Canaries*. How is it danced ?

PAVANE D'ESPAGNE

Arbeau. The *Pavane d'Espagne* is danced in moderate duple time to the air and with the movements which follow in the tabulation ; and when it has been danced in a forward direction for the first passage, the dancer must go back, retracing his steps. Then, continuing the same air, the second passage is made with new movements; then the other movements in order, which can all be learned at leisure.

Air and Movements of the *Pavane d'Espagne*

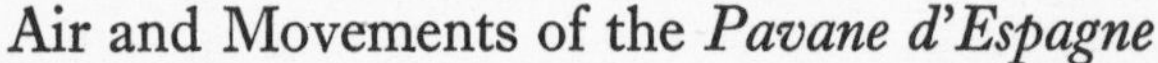

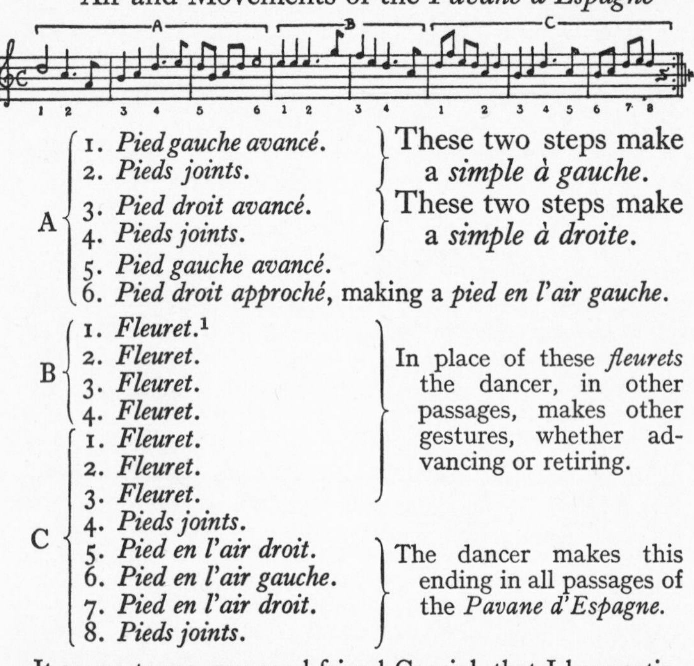

A
1. *Pied gauche avancé.*
2. *Pieds joints.*
   } These two steps make a *simple à gauche.*
3. *Pied droit avancé.*
4. *Pieds joints.*
   } These two steps make a *simple à droite.*
5. *Pied gauche avancé.*
6. *Pied droit approché*, making a *pied en l'air gauche.*

B
1. *Fleuret.*[1]
2. *Fleuret.*
3. *Fleuret.*
4. *Fleuret.*

C
1. *Fleuret.*
2. *Fleuret.*
3. *Fleuret.*
   } (B 1–4 and C 1–3) In place of these *fleurets* the dancer, in other passages, makes other gestures, whether advancing or retiring.
4. *Pieds joints.*
5. *Pied en l'air droit.*
6. *Pied en l'air gauche.*
7. *Pied en l'air droit.*
8. *Pieds joints.*
   } The dancer makes this ending in all passages of the *Pavane d'Espagne.*

It seems to me, my good friend Capriol, that I have satisfied you in telling you what I can remember of dances for war and recreation. Is it not sufficient, considering that it is such a long time since I danced and that the majority of the dances are new?

Capriol. I do not think, M. Arbeau, that it would be possible to treat of them with greater detail or lucidity. But it is true that you have again forgotten to speak of the *Bouffons.*

Arbeau. Certainly, since you have reminded me, I will tell you what I have been able to learn about it.

[1] For explanation of a *fleuret*, see p. 93.

LES BOUFFONS

The *Salii* or dancers appointed by King Numa,[1] to the number of twelve, to celebrate the sacred festivals of Mars, being dressed in painted robes with rich baldrics and pointed caps, swords at their sides, little sticks in their right hands and bucklers in their left (of which one was said to have come down from Heaven) danced to the sound of *tibiæ* and made martial gestures, sometimes successively, sometimes all together.

Capriol. Was not this the armed dance called the *Pyrrhic* which Minerva danced for joy after the defeat of the Titans ?

Arbeau. The legend says that the Curetes invented the *Pyrrhic* to entertain the infant Jupiter by their gestures and by the noise which they made by striking their swords against their bucklers. From these two dances[2] has been evolved one which is called *Bouffons* or *Mattachins*. The dancers are dressed in small corselets with ribbons on their shoulders and below their belt (the latter set off by a fringe of taffetas at the waist), morions of gilded card-board, the arms bare, bells on the legs, the sword in the right hand and the buckler in the left. These danced, with clashings of their swords and bucklers, to an air in duple time peculiar to this dance. To understand it one must know that several different gestures are made. One of these is called *feinte*, when the dancer jumps on both feet holding his sword without touching anything with it. The second is termed *estocade*, when the dancer draws back his arm and thrusts the point of his sword forward to strike that of his companion. The third is called *taille haute*, when the dancer strikes at his companion, cutting downwards with his sword from right to left. The fourth is called *revers haut*, when, on the contrary, the dancer strikes at his companion, cutting downwards

[1] Numa Pompilius, the second king of Rome, who belongs to legend and not to history. A native of Ceres, in the Sabine country, he was elected king one year after the death of Romulus. Numa's chief care was the establishment of religion among his subjects. It was he who first appointed the pontiffs, the augurs, the flamens, the chaste virgins of Vesta and the *Salii ;* the last solemnised the worship of the gods with armed dances and songs.

[2] *I.e.*, the dance of the *Salii* and the *Pyrrhic*.

from left to right. The fifth is called *taille basse*, when the dancer strikes at his companion, cutting upwards from right to left. The sixth is called *revers bas*, when he strikes at his companion, cutting upwards from left to right. And, that you may better understand the tabulation of them which I wish to give you, I shall not omit the pictures of these several gestures.

You will see above four pictures of the gestures of which I have spoken to you, that is to say, the *feinte*, *estocade*, *taille haute*, and *revers haut*. There remain the pictures of the other two gestures which you see below. Apart from these, there are still some movements of the body, but it seems to me that it will suffice for you to have these in writing without the aid of pictures.

Taille basse *Revers bas*

Capriol. Sword-play has already taught me all these gestures. Now tell me how to dance the *Bouffons*.

Arbeau. Suppose that four persons, A, B, C, D, be they soldiers or Amazons, or two of one and two of the other, suitably attired, make their entrance into the room.

Capriol. I imagine them as you say. What do they do ?

Arbeau. First, A will enter alone and, wielding his sword in time to the music, make a circle round the room and return to the entrance, placing the point of his sword against the ground as if he wished to summon his companions to combat. This done, he will recommence a Round and B will follow him, and at the end of the Round, B will summon his companions. Then A and B will make another Round, and C will follow them and do as the two others have done. Then all three will make a Round and D, who is the fourth, will follow them. And when this fourth Round is finished and there is no one else to enter, they will make a Round in the opposite direction and, at the conclusion of this, will be found formed in a group ready to begin the passages of their cuts, with the left foot forward, as they first made their Round.

D. C.

A. B.

The air of the *Bouffons* is well known to everyone. Here it is noted in its entirety and the musicians always repeat it while the Rounds and passages are being made.

Air of the *Bouffons*

Capriol. What movements will be made by the four dancers placed thus ?

Arbeau. You must know further that as long as the musicians continue to play through the air above, so the four dancers continue to dance the same movements, whether in motion when making the Rounds, or whether at rest, when making their cuts.

Capriol. Are the movements difficult to make ?

Arbeau. You will find them very easy. They are shown in the tabulation below and are danced in light duple time.

Air of the *Bouffons*

Movements for dancing the *Bouffons*

A
1. *Grue gauche.*
2. *Pied en l'air droit.*
3. *Pied en l'air gauche.*
4. *Grue droite.*
5. *Pied en l'air gauche.*
6. *Pied en l'air droit.*

B
1. *Grue gauche.*
2. *Pied en l'air droit.*
3. *Pied en l'air gauche.*
4. *Grue droite.*
5. *Pied en l'air gauche.*
6. *Pied en l'air droit.*

For as long as the dance lasts, there are no other movements but the *grues*, which take two quavers each, and two *pieds en l'air*, which take one quaver each.

You have the steps and movements of the *Bouffons ;* you will now learn the gestures which are made in the passages of cuts, which must follow immediately after the Rounds. And you must remember that at the end of a passage, a

Round must be done from left to right, with the left foot kept forward. It is then done in reverse, with the left foot kept to the rear, before beginning the passage which must follow. This is very useful to the four dancers, for while they make the Round and return, they think of a passage to do and bear it in mind. Thus, as the dancers A, B, C, D are placed, A is opposite D, and fights against him and sometimes against B, who is on his right. And similarly C will be found opposite B and will fight against him and sometimes against D. And you will note that the same gestures which A does, C must do, and thus the tabulation proper to the dancer A will serve for C, as you see below.

A fights against D and against B.	C fights against B and against D.

1. *Feinte.*	A feints with D.
2. *Taille haute.*	A attacks D.
3. *Revers haut.*	A again attacks D, then makes a three-quarter turn to the left and makes a *taille basse* at B.
4. *Taille basse.*	A turns outwards to the right, and makes a *revers bas* at B.
5. *Revers bas.*	
6. *Taille haute.*	A makes another *taille haute* against B, then makes a three-quarter turn outwards to the right, and makes a *revers bas* at D.
7. *Revers bas.*	
8. *Taille haute.*	A makes a *taille haute* at D, and changes places with D.

After A and D have changed places and C and B have also changed places at the same moment, the four will be found disposed thus :—

A. B.

D. C.

A will now fight against B and sometimes against D, and C will fight against D and sometimes against B, and perform the same gestures and cuts as above ; and when they have changed places, they will be found disposed thus :—

B. A.

C. D.

A will make the gestures, which we described at the beginning, against D and sometimes against B, as C will also do against B ; and when they have changed places, they will be found disposed thus :—

C. D.

B. A.

A will fight against B and sometimes against D ; and C against D, and sometimes against B ; and when they have changed places the dancers will be found disposed thus :—

D. C.

A. B.

You see that the four dancers are placed as they were at the beginning when their first passage is completed, and they should, without stopping, make their Round and return from it to begin the second passage, which is called the passage of the three cuts.

Capriol. I shall do the gestures of A and C well, but you have not told me what gestures D and B should make.

Arbeau. The same as A and C, and there is no difference between them except that when A and C make a three-quarter turn outwards to the left, D and B must make only a quarter turn to the right ; and when A and C make a turn outwards to the left, D and B must make the turn to the right. Other passages you will learn at your leisure.

Capriol. I shall hardly find any masters or companions who will teach me other passages, as they could other *Branles;* wherefore I pray you teach me them, for I hope some day to have a pretty masquerade for my mistress's pleasure.

Arbeau. I will gladly do so. Let us suppose, then, that the four dancers, after their Round, are disposed as at the beginning. They will then make the following passage called the passage of the three cuts.

Passage of the three cuts

A fights against D, and C against B

Air

Gestures of the second passage

Gestures	
1. *Taille haute.* 2. *Revers bas.* 3. *Taille haute.*	A makes three cuts at D then both pass to the right and change places. C does the same to B.
4. *Taille haute.* 5. *Revers bas.* 6. *Taille haute.*	A makes three cuts at B, then both pass and change places. C and D do likewise.
7. *Taille haute.* 8. *Revers bas.* 9. *Taille haute.*	A makes three cuts at D, then both pass and change places. C does the same to B.
10. *Taille haute.* 11. *Revers bas.* 12. *Taille haute.*	A makes three cuts at B, then both pass and change places. C and D do likewise, and thus the four dancers will find themselves disposed as at the beginning.

After this passage has been executed four times, the Round is made.[1]

Passage of the fifteen cuts

Air

Gestures of the third passage

1. *Taille haute.* — A, head turned inwards, attacks D, whose head is turned outwards.
2. *Revers bas.* — A attacks B, whose head is turned outwards.
3. *Taille haute.* — A against D again.
4. *Revers bas.* — A against B again.
5. *Taille haute.* — A, head turned outwards, attacks B, whose head is turned inwards.

[1] It must be clearly understood that each passage is executed four times in succession before proceeding to a new passage.

6. *Revers bas.*	A attacks D, whose head is turned inwards.
7. *Taille haute.*	A attacks B again.
8. *Revers bas.*	A attacks D again.
1. *Taille haute.*	A, head turned inwards, attacks D, whose head is turned outwards.
2. *Revers bas.*	A attacks B, whose head is turned outwards.
3. *Taille haute.*	A against D again.
4. *Revers bas.*	A against B again.
5. *Taille haute.*	A, head turned outwards, attacks B, whose head is turned inwards.
6. *Revers bas.*	A attacks D, whose head is turned inwards.
7. *Taille haute.*	A attacks B. Both pass to the right and change places.

This done, A, head turned outwards, attacks D, whose head is turned inwards, the entire passage being executed four times in all.

Passage called Estocade

After the Round is made, the four dancers are found disposed as at the beginning.

Air

Gestures of the fourth passage

1. *Taille haute.*	A attacks D, and C attacks B.
2. *Revers haut.*	A attacks D again, and C attacks B again.
3. *Taille basse.*	A attacks D again, and C attacks B again.
4. *Coude retiré.* 5. *Estocade.*	All four, A, B, C and D draw back their elbows and clash their bucklers together.
6. *Taille haute.*	A attacks D, and C attacks B.
7. *Revers haut.*	A attacks D again, and C attacks B again.

8. *Taille basse.*
9. *Coude retiré.*
10. *Estocade.*

} A attacks D and C attacks B, then all four draw back their elbows, clash their bucklers together, pass to the right and change places.

A will now fight against B, and D against C. When the passage has been executed four times, the dancers will be found disposed as at the beginning.

Passage called Bastion

Air

Gestures of the fifth passage

Suppose that the dancers are placed as at the beginning, D and B will place themselves back to back.

1. *Taille haute.*	A against D, and C against B.
2. *Revers bas.*	A against B, and C against D.
3. *Taille haute.*	A against D, and C against B. All pass and change places.
4. *Taille haute.*	A against B, and C against D.
5. *Revers bas.*	A against D, and C against B.
6. *Taille haute.*	A against B, and C against D. All pass and change places.
7. *Taille haute.*	A against D, and C against B.
8. *Revers bas.*	A against B, and C against D.
9. *Taille haute.*	A against D, and C against B. All pass and change places.
10. *Taille haute.*	A against B, and C against D.
11. *Revers bas.*	A against D, and C against B.
12. *Taille haute.*	A against B, and C against D. All pass and change places.

When the passage has been executed four times, the four dancers will be found disposed as at the beginning. Then, without intermission, they make their Rounds as described already, to prepare for the sixth passage.

Passage called The Hay

Air

Gestures of the sixth passage

1. *Taille haute.* A attacks D, and C attacks B. Both pass to their right and change places.
2. *Revers bas.* A attacks B, and C attacks D. Both pass and change places.
3. *Taille haute.* A attacks D, and C attacks B. Both pass and change places.
4. *Revers bas.* A attacks B, and C attacks D. Both pass and change places, and find themselves disposed as at the beginning.
5. *Taille haute.* A attacks D, and C attacks B. Both pass and change places as above.
6. *Revers bas.* A attacks B, and C attacks D. Both pass and change places.
7. *Taille haute.* A attacks D, and C attacks B. Both pass and change places.
8. *Revers bas.* A attacks B, and C attacks D. Both pass and change places, and find themselves disposed as at the beginning.

You must now reverse the Hay, which will leave A against B, and C against D, when it is done. They will then repeat the Hay as before, and its reverse, and, when all this is done, will be found disposed as at the beginning. They will then retire.

Capriol. M. Arbeau, I thank you for the trouble you have taken in teaching me to dance.

Arbeau. I should like to have been able to make the result equal to the wealth of my sincere affection for you. In the future I hope to give you the airs and movements of several ballets and masquerades which have taken place in this town. We will deal with these in a second treatise [1] as soon as we have leisure to do so. However, practise these

[1] This intention was not fulfilled.

dances carefully and you will become a fit companion of the planets, which dance of their own nature, and of those Nymphs whom Marcus Varro said he had seen in Lydia come out of a pool and dance to the sound of flutes, and then return to their pool. And when you have danced with your mistress you will return to the great pool of your studies and gain profit from it, as I pray God give you grace to do.

INDEX OF SUBJECTS

INDEX OF SUBJECTS

INDEX OF SUBJECTS

INDEX OF SUBJECTS

INDEX OF SUBJECTS

INDEX OF AIRS

INDEX OF NAMES

INDEX OF NAMES